Life
Living in Fantastic Energy

Taking Charge of Your Thoughts and Ideas and
Harnessing the Law of Expression and Attraction

Rev Craig M Harris

Copyright © 2014 Authored By Rev Craig M Harris
All rights reserved.

ISBN: 1500276332
ISBN 13: 9781500276331
Library of Congress Control Number: 2014911463
CreateSpace Independent Publishing Platform
North Charleston, South Carolina

A special thanks to Rev. Mary Emma Dryden; my wife, Adele Zydel Harris; and Lisa Van Ahn for their creative input and suggestions.

Thank you to all my teachers, friends, and students.
A gratitude of thanks to Rev. Lucia Faugno, Dr. Rev. Al Salazar, Rev. Janet Friedline, Rev. Donna Gatewood, Mr. Wayne Gatewood, Dr. Rev. Maurita Wiggins, Dr. Rev. Miriam Comer Johnson, Rev. Eric Butterworth, Rev. Olga Butterworth, Rev. Justin Epstein, Richard Chambers, Connie Falconi, Michael Rappaport, Maureen (Pinky) Urban, and again to my wife Adele Zydel Harris.

As the wind blows through the trees, and we hear the wind blowing through the trees....
we hear each leafs individual experience of the wind.
One tree and yet each leaf is of its own self having its own motion and reaction from the wind...
We are of one God, one Mind, personal and yet impersonal. Life is....God is....I am.....
We are one, individually, indivisibly, in expression and experience...
We are children of peace, wisdom, grace, joy, love, wellness, and life.
I Am that I Am.

Rev. Craig M. Harris

I would like to dedicate this book in memory to my parents

Jean Macdonald Harris
for her strong and good heart

David Allen Harris
I believe with all my heart that several days
after he had passed on, he stopped by
and left in me all his good and positive traits

I Love You Mom and Dad

Awakening to Our Innate Potential

Infinity within is something so powerful waiting for us to harness and express in all its divine glory. Tapping into this awareness, we can begin a path of undoing in order to move forth and an unlearning in order to understand, practice, and make manifest through our true innate self. We are divine in nature. It is our purpose to receive and express the goodness of our Creator. We are meant to make manifest the well-being of creation; to experience it, create in it and of it, abundantly in infinite wellness.

Often I have questioned why one thing is so important to one person and yet means nothing to another other? Why do we hold steadfast to our ideas? Do we often limit ourselves to what we think and who we are? Can we change simply because we truly want to? The list goes on.

I now know that we can take charge of all our thoughts and ideas. It takes discipline and a mindful awareness of what and why we do what we do.

For the truth is, with every thought we have we attach an emotion to it. And that emotion can inspire us or tear us down. But we do make that decision. We are in charge. No matter how deeply we are influenced, after all is said and done, we make the final decision. No one else can do that for us.

So, first you must ask yourself: Am I really being forced into the decisions I am making? Can I begin to change these thoughts to a certain degree or even entirely? Have I been reckless and easily swayed by menial practices that appear to be of great importance and power, but are perhaps limited and minuscule? Do I feel like I am being held back by these influences, that there is something deep inside me that is wonderful and wants to come out?

Often we are influenced by illusions and erroneous thoughts of great limitations.

If you have even a notion that you have been going down that path then perhaps this is a beginning for you. A beginning that is awakening you from the "*race mind" that moves us around like cattle and dictates to us: what to eat, what to wear, what to listen to, what to watch, what to think, and what to believe.

We are so much more than that. We are creative, intelligent, soulful beings. We are spiritual beings having a human experience. We have our beautiful innate self that is filled with the wisdom of all life eternal and infinite in goodness, waiting to illuminate us and fulfill us with a destiny that is ours to take charge in.

There is no better moment than the moment you're in to begin to discover your true self and *live in fantastic energy.*

Peace and Blessings,
Craig Harris

Race mind - Absorbing, ingesting, obsessing, and being influenced and constricted to the erroneous thought of the self-will. An extreme lack of the innate self. The inability to know peace and practice grace and wisdom in what we say and do. Believing in separation, good vs. bad, right vs. wrong, etc.

**Often I use the word God. Some struggle with this name...this sound. I have learned to redefine it. For me it carries the deepest, most high aspirations of enlightenment and illumination. There is not a hint of anthropomorphism to be found in this word. I also use* *words such as Light of Life, Universal Presence, Divine Mind, Creator, Omnipresent Parent, Mother/Father, Infinite Mind, One Mind, and All-Inclusive Love. All these words convey only goodness, love, wisdom, peace, grace, creativity, and power in the most highest form of positive thinking and living.*

Contents

Chapter One: Peace Is Still a Good Idea…But Where Is It?	1
Chapter Two: Self-Will…Highly Overrated and Delusional	10
Chapter Three: We Live What We Vibrate	20
Chapter Four: Smile and Love	26
Chapter Five: Where Is Now?	35
Chapter Six:	
Part One: That Fiery Inferno, That Bottomless Pit…The Subconscious	
Part Two: Four Laws of Living in Fantastic Energy	44
• The Law of Surrender	48
• The Law of Mind	50
• The Law of Expression	52
• The Law of Attraction	54
Chapter Seven: One Creative Thought: I Am	58
Chapter Eight: Altering My Gifts Before the Altar	67
Chapter Nine: Surrender to Win	78
Chapter Ten: Life…Living in Fantastic Energy	86
Bibliography	91

one
Peace Is Still a Good Idea...But Where Is It?

> *John 14:27*
> *Peace I leave you with, my own Peace I give*
> *you, a peace the world cannot give...*

> *Romans 6:14*
> *For sin shall not have dominion over you: for ye*
> *are not under the law, but under grace.*

Most of us are wrapped up in the human world; a world where we have been given self-will to think and create. Where we believe all the answers are found through man's self-glorifying achievements. But our temporary kingdom is only temporary stuff of the material world. The more things we can accumulate, the more powerful we become—for a while. But there's that never-ending hunger, that emptiness: there are always others who in some way, somehow have more. And then there are those who want to ruin and take from those who accumulate massive amounts of stuff.

For a short time we find contentment in our newfound things. We find pleasure—a false sense of security with feelings of power.

And then there's love...or is it really just lust after all? We are constantly lusting for all man's temporary ideas. Running ourselves crazy, keeping up the front, but behind closed doors, we're on the road to losing it. Flying high and yet at the same time feeling sad and miserable; making ourselves sick with illness and disease, with drugs, alcohol, gambling, and sex, and putting people down just so we can feel big about ourselves so we can accumulate more of the latest fads and technology and even, perhaps, a little extra time.

Our pride tells us we're just fine in our temporary world, surviving in all of these wonderful illusions. Our ego is pleased, but with what? Artificial stimulants, self-indulgence, and delusions, and denying ourselves True Peace, True Grace, True Wisdom, and True Love. We are in the image of God but blindly building beautiful things and often feeding our creativity with envy, jealousy, paranoia, anger, rage, distrust, disharmony, hatred, and greed. We construct as we self-destruct.

Yes, our pride tells us we don't need to change or even look at ourselves. Pride, ego, and self-centeredness remain at the helm of our delusional thinking. Brilliance and education end up being some of our fiercest walls to hide behind.

There is a beautiful universe, right here, right now. It is the stuff we are made of. Its wisdom is what we are. The kingdom of God is here on earth, within all life. Nothing can exist without God's Wisdom. That Innate Intelligence is already within us. It is how we are built, and it is what energizes our entire being.

Some go on about the big bang theory. Well, every seed that gives root has a big bang within itself. That big bang is the stuff that is God's Wisdom in action making manifest, and it is good. The big bang is explained in Genesis. It is the seven days of creation. This explanation is not a time in history documenting what was. It is about what God does. The seven days of creation is about the timeless moment of now in ceaseless creation. In other words, it is about everything. From the seed that sprouts, a shoot that grows into a form of life with deliberate purpose, to the stuff that makes the spiritual being who is here on earth for a deliberate purpose.

We have more to do than just scurry around, trapped with misguided devotion to the fads and technology of the moment. Yes we are made to make manifest but while putting God Consciousness first in all that we do. Putting God first is in and of itself a prayer that will never fail.

We are first spiritual beings. Here on earth we have a temple where we dwell. It is not vegetable or mineral, it is not just an electron or a proton; it is animal. We are the tenants and God is the landlord. God supplies us with all we need and yet that often goes ignored. His perfection is with us, for we are an expression of God, but our mind filters it down with our illusions and erroneous thoughts as we desperately grasp at the outer world looking for it to fix us, and in turn setting ourselves up to the vulnerability of the quick fixes that die out fast and leave us in dire straits

A woman I worked with had suffered greatly with depression her whole life. During her childhood she had many visits to hospitals as they kept reevaluating her condition and the medications to give her. This continued into her adulthood. Though a very successful business woman, she, nonetheless, was still on high doses of medication.

We had begun a study together focusing on our true innate spiritual selves rather than our physical, educated selves. Meditation was a major factor with this path.

She began to realize that her search for God had to stop. Instead she began to realize her deep inner self that was already one with God. She mentioned that she was experiencing a beautiful peace and grace in daily living. That continued to increase, and as it did, for the first time in her life, her medication began to decrease.

By the time we had finished our spiritual journey, she was off 90 percent of her medication. I should note her decrease of medication was under her doctor's guidance.

I have spoken with her a couple of times since, and she continues on the new journey and spending time in the silence of meditation, allowing her innate self to make manifest in her daily living. In doing so God's Grace and Peace continue to grow and flow through her.

God just is; I Am that I Am, all good. All these things that we feel we need in our lives are an expression of God in action, but only an expression. They are not the source; they are the effect but not the cause. They will come, and they will go. They are temporary in expression, but we are not and neither is God.

We are creative spiritual beings having a human experience. It is our true spiritual selves that we need to put first, not our humanness. It is when we put first things first that we find the True Peace that we are seeking. Living in abundance is what God wants for us. But we must truly ask ourselves, "Am I living in abundance or am I just hoarding and consuming, trying to fill the emptiness that never seems to quite go away? Am I constantly trying to reconnect to happiness through the outer world ignoring the inner world of my divine true nature?"

Often mankind is trying to achieve on the outside to fill that emptiness within. This practice is actually taught to us through numerous books, the media, and the educational system.

I'm not claiming they are wrong. In man's world, there are great, even brilliant ideas that have led to incredible success stories on how to accumulate a lot of material wealth and do a lot of fun things. All that is great, but it is temporary and it is not the source of peace—of True Peace that can be found within. The peace we seek comes from within and must come first.

To wait for God to show up when He is already here clearly states that one is not looking rightly. We already have that peace within us. To seek the outer world for its temporary moments of peace is like a man in the desert hoping to come upon an oasis. But to have God's Peace, to be conscious of it working through you, expressing from your soul, is the vibration you will live in and express from. In other words, your cup will runneth over.

God is omnipresent, both personal and impersonal. He is equally expressing through you, equally as He is through all of life. For all that exists is God in creative action. From Elohim to Jehovah, the invisible God of conscious thought, to the manifestation of idea formed in spiritual matter, all is spiritual. All is God. Matter is just a slower vibration, a slower frequency wave of God's Mind.

Some claim if they can't see it, it doesn't exist. Well then good luck breathing. Air is invisible. You know it's there; your senses acknowledge it.

The same is true of the creative infinite Parent. If you take the time to experience truth, you will not be able to deny it anymore. Just like breathing, it is real. One must wake up from the illusions and erroneous thoughts that guide one throughout the day in an extremely limited awareness of life

The God of my understanding is compassionate, all loving, all caring, nonblaming, all healing, and all wise. All God asks is to be included in our lives. The so-called jealous, angry, and condemning God is just us messing ourselves up in the false thought that we are separate from God and looking to put the blame elsewhere. We just need to let God do God's Work, and we will know what we're supposed to be doing.

Often man can do things with the best of intentions and yet only be adding fuel to the fire simply because we are trying to do God's Work.

I have met with people, who have very successful careers except for one snag, they are very unhappy with what they are doing. They had been literally forced into their work. Often by guilt and fear, and people manipulating them for their own good. Often the best of intentions have paved a road with destruction and ruin.

It is best that when we pray for others we just hold them in the light, and see them as perfect and well. We should not ask God to give them this or to give them that. God already knows, we don't need to tell Him. If we must talk, we can simply say, "Father / Mother, may my prayer of love be a conscious part of your plan, and my true and only desire is that they may awaken to the path that is theirs, through you, to have." Amen.

Mother Teresa put it quite simply, "If you sincerely want to learn to pray: keep silence." Note she says silence not silent. Take a moment here to contemplate on this before continuing.

It comes down to trust and faith; two very powerful tools. Opposing a thing is to still be a part of it. Though it is an opposite, it is still a part of it. Christ Jesus told us to resist not evil. Walk into the light not the darkness.

When we turn within to the Father and know His Peace we also begin to know His Wisdom. We must go to Him in the silence, to be still, to pause, and to enter into a place where the Spirit of Life speaks to us. That place where Jesus went to when he communed with the Father in Christ Mind. A place that Paul tells us over and over "is within us all." For God is everything, and God, expressing through us all, does so in the Sonship of Christ Consciousness. It is our bridge in oneness with our Father who art in heaven. This is where our peace dwells: infinitely in God's strength, the fountainhead that runneth over eternally for each and every one of us who choose to do so.

We can ruin ourselves over luxury problems: we don't have enough, it's not good enough, we want to look better than the next person, there's a scratch on the new car. This is being lost in that muck and mire of man's idea of life.

In truth, we are whole in Spirit. That cannot change. God does not change; God will not move the axis of the universe every time the king and queen baby within foolishly lay demands and contracts before God.

Often we are quick to draw conclusions and have an answer to go with them when in truth we have no idea of what God's plan is. That plan is perfect. Just because I don't understand doesn't mean it's no good; it means I don't understand.

The peace I have found from communing with God, from knowing there is no separation from God, and that the Father and I are one is taught throughout the Bible, especially in the final book, Revelation. When I am right with God I know that God's plan is perfect, which for me requires daily communing with God.

We are bombarded with many illusions and erroneous thoughts, and we look and listen to all of them. We have made many of them, and as they have been passed on to generation after generation, they have become thicker and wider but never deeper. Untruth cannot go deep, for it is shallow. However, in the world of illusions, it can make a big mess as it spreads itself.

In the Bible it talks of inheriting the sins of past generations. (Deuteronomy 5:9, Exodus 34:7, Numbers 14:18, 1 Samuel 3:12–13, Jeremiah 16:10, and the list goes on and on.) Simply, what is being said here is that we inherit what we ignore. We accept it as, "Well, this is just the way things are." If you believe that, then that is exactly what you'll get.

The Bible also explains this in many passages: Second Kings 14:6, "But the children of the murderers he slew not: according unto that which is written in the book of the law of Moses, wherein the Lord commanded, saying, The fathers shall not be put to death for the children, nor the children be put to death for the fathers; but every man shall be put to death for his own sin." Jeremiah 31:29–30, "In those days they shall say no more, 'The fathers have eaten a sour grape, and the children's teeth are set on edge.' But every one shall die for his own iniquity."

For in truth our power is simply this: Romans 6:14, "For sin shall not have dominion over you: for ye are not under the law, but under grace."

Prejudice is a perfect example. How we look at one another without love. God is love and we are in the image of God. God is not fear, but often the human being uses fear to extrapolate solutions. In doing so, a lot of pollution is generated from one mind to the other.

My working with incarcerated men can only come from God's Grace. Anything less than that and I would be unwelcome there. Many of the people I have met there have very deep spiritual beliefs and many of them have deep wisdom.

We may be in this world, but we are not of it. We are of God. We are His children. We are in His Likeness. We are the inheritors of His Kingdom, His Wisdom, His Glory, His Love, and His Peace. It is not something we hope to have someday. His Kingdom is here now. God is with us for He is us in action, expressing in absolute goodness. We can live up to His Divine plan for it is our true nature to do so. The illusions we live in are a false belief of duality and separation, more popularly known as evil. For duality is the original sin. We are not followers, we are one.

The sun does not rise or set; it shines as the earth rotates. Nor does the sun break through the clouds, the clouds dissipate. We are not followers of Christ; we are of Christ Mind and one with our Creator for we are His Creative thought and he expresses through us with us, being us, as is, and fills us with love, peace, and wisdom for He is love, peace, and wisdom. Therefore we are love, peace, and wisdom in action, in constant expression.

So why do we come up short? Why are we so attracted to the temporary illusions? Why do we make ourselves sick? Why do we blame others? Why are we spinning out of control when we are in the likeness of our Creator? The upcoming chapters will take a deeper look into these questions. For now, one can immediately start to hit the spiritual brakes. Take time to know that God is love and so are you. God is peace and so are you. God is health and so are you. God is abundance and so are you. God is wisdom and so are you.

Lesson (Guidelines)

God is all good and omnipresent, omniscient, and omnipotent. Wherever you are, so is God. God is I Am and God is, and I am. There is no separation, we are one.

- Take the time to reflect on this and then take time for prayer and meditation.
- Spend time in silence, let what ever happens, happen, If you sway into thought, just return to the silence. At this stage do not be frustrated or concerned with how little time you spend in silence or how often you have to return. "Be still and know that I am God.", in its simplicity is infinite. So to experience even a moment is to experience the infinite, and a lot can happen in that moment. Again, just sit back, relax, and let whatever happens, happen
- Slow down your breathing. Inhale saying to yourself I am, pause for a few seconds and exhale, saying to yourself spirit. You can choose another word such as peace, love, well, etc.
- Listen to the silence and be receptive to it. It is the language of life eternal.

Selah (Pause for silence)
Peace be with you...for it already is, and so it is.
Amen

two

Self-Will...Highly Overrated and Delusional

Mark 10:18
So Jesus said to him, 'Why do you call me good?
No one is good but One, that is, God.'

The moon shines bright on a night like tonight. It helps bring light to the dark night, romance in the air, and poetry to the ears. So how does the moon shine? It is but the reflection of the sun, bouncing the light of the sun out into the universe.

Self-will is like moonlight, although we have free will, to choose it is still the will of God. It is God's will that we have self-will but that will is of God, it is not ours alone. It is a misunderstood statement, like the sun rises and the sun sets. We live in the illusion that we are separate from God. This illusion only leads to a consistent recurrence of shortcomings, dysfunctional behaviors, bad habits, addictions, and a regular ongoing practice of taking the Lord's name in vain.

When Moses asked, "Who are you," the answer was straight forward, "I Am that I Am."

God is I Am and God is and I am. The I Am being God Omnipresent, Omniscient, and Omnipotent; both personal and impersonal. The I am is ourselves as one with God Omnipresent, Omniscient, and

Omnipotent, but it is personal. We are one with God. There is no separation. Often when we refer to "I am" we use it recklessly and in vain. There is no spiritual healing in a statement like, "I am no good" or "I am sick," etc. This is taking the Lord's name in vain. In vain simply means to do something with no good coming from it.

I am is a very powerful tool. Used correctly it can immediately lift you up into a higher more spiritually fit state of mind, and in turn begin to make a difference in your daily life that is healthy and more gratifying. I am good, I am healthy, I am wise, I am happy, I am filled with joy. We have dominion over our negativity but it requires a steady practice, just as it requires a steady practice to function in a negative way that will bring about disease, sickness, and illnesses.

I am is the chosen name God has given to us all and God is the "I" of I am. We need not dwell in some false belief that we are on the outside looking in. We are as much of the within as the without. There is no separation. Everything is Spirit.

The original sin is to believe that we are separate from God. It sends us into a direction that is extremely limited and narrow. In this delusional state of mind, we think that God is in the image of us instead of the truth that we are in the image of God.

In disconnecting we consistently make demands and present petitions to God rather than just clearing our side of the street and knowing that in God all is well.

Often when I sense that my life is off kilter, I will take the time and become aware of what unnecessary thoughts have been going on in my head and what kind of emotion I'm attaching to it. Often I find the demands in my head are unrealistic or I've been building up resentment. Some sort of fear is often buried in there, always under the anger. So I get honest and ask myself, "Is this the state of mind

I really want to be in? Is this going to really be useful in helping with what I'm trying to achieve? Is this a part of God Mind? Isn't God Mind the most powerful way to live?

God is good. All that God made is good, it is perfection. Often human beings struggle to live in this false belief creating separation and constantly asking God instead of simply saying thank you for your wisdom here on earth and thank you that I'm aware of my shortcomings and can, once again, let them go!

Our thoughts are our prayers, and in the divine order of life, our thoughts are being made manifest. When we take the time to sit in silence and give thanks in a consciousness of gratitude then we begin to bring forth God's Wisdom and abundance from within and make manifest from the Kingdom of Heaven.

A kingdom that is here and now heaven is all that is, and earth is from the allness of heaven, for it is God's creation. As it is clearly stated, "Our Father which art in heaven hallowed be thy name, thy kingdom come <u>thy will be done on earth as it is in heaven."</u>

So why do we as a people not seize this blessed truth and live within it expressing in the grace of God's Wisdom and Harmony?

The world is filled with ignorance of chaos, deceit, corruption, distrust, sorrow, vengeance, bitterness, jealousy, hatred, and violence.

We are surrounded by it everywhere we go, and so we are easily manipulated/influenced by it. We create our own locusts and scorpions coming up from that bottomless pit of our subconscious that fills the air and burns our nostrils.

It is living in the delusion of separation that keeps us in torment and constantly pulling from the outer world to feel good about ourselves. We are not vacuum cleaners sucking up everything we possibly can; we are creative beings in the image of our Mother/Father.

This bottomless pit called our subconscious can be hellish if we do not live in the truth that we have dominion over the earth. The earth is our outer manifestation from our expression. So how do we express and in that expression what becomes attracted to our daily living?

I know a woman who had been out of work for a while. She finally stopped with the suggestions on how to find a job and put her trust in God. In God's way and in God's time and all was well. Soon after she was invited to go on a cruise with a friend of hers who offered to treat. She decided to go. She had mentioned that if she was not practicing living in God's Goodness she would not have let herself go, given her situation. She went on the cruise and had a wonderful time. While doing so she made a connection for a job interview that was what she was looking for. After her vacation, she went on the interview and was hired.

Self-will can be so insidious in erroneous thought that we can make it look believable as if we are dealing with our problems in a positive way by taking a stand, making a difference, and being responsible, yet all the while all we're doing is feeding and nourishing the problem. These same problems keep showing up over and over again. Sometimes they are unrecognizable, but in truth they are the same old same old.

Resist not evil is the key to living a harmonious life (Matthew 5:39, 48, "But I say unto you, That ye resist not evil: but whosoever shall smite thee on thy right cheek, turn to him the other also…Be ye therefore perfect, even as your Father which is in heaven is perfect."). Fighting in man's outer world is not the solution. Living in God's Wisdom is. It is there that we turn the problems over to God. It is God's battle not ours. Our work is to live steadfast in God's Grace (Peace, Love, Wisdom, Knowledge, Joy, Life); to remain diligent in ceaseless prayer.

I have been working in a jail with some of the incarcerated men. They have, on their own, a Bible study. Many of them are sharing their understanding of "resist not evil." Instead of always feeling a need to step up to every situation and resolving the immediate problem with little regard to the outcome, or just saying whatever goes down, goes down, many are turning their problems over to God. They are accepting that these struggles are God's battles not theirs.

Our battles are not with battling it out with evil, but instead with not getting tangled up in it, even with the best of intentions. To fight it is to still be a part of it.

That is still living in the erroneous thought of duality. There is only one mind and one power, and that is God.

Taking time on a daily basis for prayer and meditation is essential to keeping us right-minded. However, we do not necessarily have to spend all day on our knees with our heads bowed. There is a time and place for everything. To remain in ceaseless prayer is to do one's best to be conscious of our thoughts and how they are directing us. This is the one place God has given us to do what we will with our thoughts.

All our thoughts are prayer for there is only One Mind. We average several thousand thoughts per day.

In right thinking comes right expression and in return right attraction. The universe functions on the oneship of intake outtake. The way the planets turn, the way a seed sprouts a stem, the way water moves, the way we breathe, the way we love. The same principle: a continuum of the allness of life expressing and attracting, over and over, in and of the same principle: one energy, one vibration, one creative thought: Love Supreme.

Our thoughts, though they are our own, they nonetheless are one with the All Being, All Science, and All Powerful Parent, which is life all good.

How often are our minds filled with the self-will of negativity? The tragedy is that we are intelligent people and yet we fill our minds with ignorance (doubt, mistrust, deceit, resentments, bitterness, conceit, hatred, vengeance, confusion).

God is all good and there is no place for erroneous thinking.

This is a lack of <u>truth</u> not of <u>faith</u>, for our faith is always strong. It's in the erroneous thought that we begin living in the delusion of self-will and self-will alone. Our faith becomes horribly poisoned of our own doing. To keep blaming others, situations, or life itself is to stay in a state of mind that is self-centered, and egotistical, full of mankind's outer personality, and feeling quite empty on the inside. It is pride in reverse.

In this state of acceptance our faith turns to faith in nothing working right, faith in fear, faith in doubt, faith in worry, faith in vengeance, faith in not forgiving, faith in lack, and faith in not believing in oneself. Yes, faith always remains strong.

I have been making a point in keeping truth very loud in my head. Rather than letting the noise of the daily accumulated strife wreak havoc in my head. I have been creating a practice of acknowledging my true innate self, turning up the volume, and declaring God's love and peace, knowing the outer chaos of erroneous thought is of no use to me.

It works rather well. I recommend trying it out. Give it a chance. It's a practice, and I know for myself practicing takes time to develop its great potential.

To live in the midst of God is to live in the energy of love all powerful. There is nothing more powerful than Divine Love Supreme. Destruction is only a lack of love being expressed and so the attraction is destruction. Destruction has an illusion of being powerful. But it has no power. That is why destruction expresses in a form of damage. What makes it powerful is it's powerlessness.

It is an error of illusion appearing as life in separation. It cannot overpower love for it has no power. God is the only power. It has no energy that is why it hurts. It is not our nature to be powerless and void of energy.

God is omnipresent, omniscient, and omnipotent or God is not. It cannot be both ways. Destruction is the false absence of God. It is an abomination in thought to have severely filtered God Mind or the innate mind to a trickle of primitive animalistic expression, allowing only intellect to conclude and guide us. This is disharmony from within the self. God can only express good. God Mind can be altered. The shining moon has no light of its own but it reflects and refracts the sun's light, and that light moves in accordance to the moon's motion.

All that we need is already there, complete. God is not a part of wickedness, sickness, or disease. It is only our thoughts and ideas that create these things. Evil is not a power for God to reckon with. Evil is only the immaturity and ignorance brought on from the fear, envy, vengeance, unforgiveness, and jealousy of self-centeredness.

God's will be done, not mine, is the cry of the being who is growing more into the likeness of our Creator. But let's take this a step further into simplicity and just say God's will be done!

We are in the midst of God's absolute goodness. The struggles, the agony, and the hurt are of our doing. The ideas may have been passed on to us to a certain degree, but all the more to consider this thought: "Are these really my thoughts...my beliefs?" Why stay there when we don't have to? The need to stay in such consciousness is a form of sickness that will repeat itself over and over only because we choose to stay in it. Justification can be a very harmful reasoning to continue staying stuck.

Often this requires patience. It's not uncommon to go in and out of it. Letting go often requires letting go over and over. This in and of itself is discipline. When we are truly ready to let go, we will. I have been amazed at how long I can hold on to something that I believe I don't want anymore. Something, however, deep within me still can't quite come into agreement. Fear is always at the helm in this situation. Trust often builds slowly, especially unto our own selves.

For years I denied myself the truth of going into ministry. Who am I to be a minister? (That's a big one, fear and pride in reverse; a negative ego.) I don't have the time or the means. How will I make a living? It's too late! I should have done it years ago! This is just wishful thinking; pipe dreams with an inner voice proclaiming, "Get your head out of the clouds!" (Which is not my voice but an inherited statement.)

However, if I am on God's path as one, then all is well. I often find these so-called coincidences keep aligning into place to create a path that is mine to take. No matter how deep the water, there is rock under my feet allowing me to gracefully, perhaps drudging at times as I learn, but gracefully going forth on my journey, my adventure. Matthew 5:48, "Be ye therefore perfect, even as your Father which is in heaven is perfect." We are perfect beings in search of perfection. Ideally we learn as we go along.

We can let go and trust the notion that perhaps there is something greater at work here, and put our faith in a more positive direction in the meaning to the words, "We have dominion over the earth (*that final expression in life)." If you can't find it within you to do so, then how about just giving it the benefit of the doubt? To really give it a chance, not just a whim or a quick glance, but to really make some room within and see where it goes. To have dominion over the earth is about us. We do have dominion over ourselves for we are children of light and that light is God (no separation). It is God's strength, might, and power that are working through us, expressing as us.

We are light and our faith, which is the activity of God always working in us, can bring forth the Spirit of Life (Holy Spirit), revealing it's wisdom to us and manifesting into thought and into creative expression.

We are both spiritual and human beings, invisible and visible. We are life in motion. There is so much more to us than just our flesh here on earth. We are perfect beings searching for perfection.

In the story of Eden, there is a land called Nod. What is being said here is that, even in the consciousness of Eden, one can be continually nodding and dozing, taking a nap from life while one goes about his or her business and slowly drift away from truly living in life itself; to walk aimlessly. That sounds very sad, actually. We are quite capable of going through life self-hypnotized with a smile and a gleam in the eye.

To wake up is a true blessing. Often there are many awakenings within awakenings and repeated reawakenings.

God's will be done only means for me to live fully as who I am. To keep practicing and keep learning Divine Wisdom and expressing it in the grace and joy of our true beings; to keep returning to the wellness of our Cosmic Parent, God, is to continue living in the purposeful presence of our lives, untouched, unblemished, heavenly divine, supreme, and unstoppable in the eternal moment.

Do not fear it is only I. I am light infinite, eternal, all good, all well. I am love. I am life. I am expression in motion.
Do not fear. You are one. You are light infinite, eternal, all good, all well. You are love, life, and expression in motion. I am always with you. Be still and know that I Am God.

Lesson (Guidelines)

- Check in on your mental and emotional state a few times a day. It can make a big difference.
- Ask yourself, Where am I emotionally and spiritually?

- Is it really the state of mind you want to be in?
  (It becomes so easy to feed off fear and anger and resentments in order to get through the day.)
- You can always stop and start the day over, even if it's the end of the day; even if starting over occurs several or many times in a given day.
- Know that you are tapped into an infinite source of absolute goodness and wellness. Allow yourself to get out of the way of your own self. Stop the thoughts and allow the emotions to simmer down.
- Acknowledge to yourself, "I am restored to that which never left, that which is in harmony with a purposeful state of well-being. The outer negativity is not mine and I need not indulge myself in it. I am seeking the solution by being the solution. I am peace, I am wellness, I am receptive to my highest good, and forgive all encounters that have accorded today, be it from others or even from my own self. I forgive."

Peace

The final expression in life: *First there is consciousness, then followed by imagination. Imagination becomes a creative idea that is then brought into manifestation. The final step in life is the outer experience that began with consciousness.*

three

We Live What We Vibrate

John 1:1,14
In the beginning was the word...full of Grace and Truth.
John 1:5
And the light shines in the darkness, and the
darkness did not comprehend it.

We feed our soul and we live off the vibration of our soul. There's no way around that. We can change what we feed our soul. We have dominion. After all is said and done, we make the decision about how to react to every situation. It is easy to fall prey to going forth with sarcasm, wit and other forms of intellectual superiority; physical strength of various degrees is encouraged while meekness and humility are often frowned upon or just overlooked. Faith is often frowned upon or remains on the back burner when compared to pride and ego.

Why use faith at all? It seems no matter how prideful or self-assured we become there is that need for inner strength that we find or, for some, hope for in faith. So why use it a little bit, turn to it a little, or ignore it unless we're desperate?

Faith does not make God work in us. Faith is the activity of God already at work in us. We do not pray to God but from the consciousness of God.

Veils and illusions are deceiving. We can be carried on the wave of erroneous thoughts and fairy-tale beliefs as long as a brutal reality doesn't come a knocking. When it does, all illusions suddenly seem unimportant. How quickly, though, the human psyche is to forget once the problem dissipates. How easy to fall back into the soft comforts of a life; to live in an illusion of feeling full but in truth living malnourished, succumbing to temporary outer pleasures in a universe designed to give us our daily bread within and without.

To give us our daily bread is a guarantee to work the way the universe has been designed: in an abundance of goodness. Divine Goodness. This completion of the true self is an awakening in the understanding that we are in the image and likeness of our Creator. Often people think their supply channels are investments, employers, businesses, or even energy fields of certain conducts. And though great results can come from them, where do these channels stem from? They are only pathways, even great and needed pathways, but are often recognized in and only of themselves. There is only one source. There is no separation; it is our reason for health and happiness. In this awareness, our journey only brightens in the unfoldment of our ever evolving self. We require freedom. It is in claiming this freedom that we are fulfilled, from food to prayer, from material to illumination, from inner substance to outer substance, from invisible to visible, from knowledge to wisdom, and from negative to positive. It is there that we are provided all that we need to live and to live well. Whether we realize it or not, practice it or not, believe in it or not, truth remains truth. We can work oblivious to it or enlightened by it. Truth is an unchangeable spirit, and to know this truth—truly know it with all of one's mind, body, heart, and strength—is to know all is well and all is good.

When one realizes that God is the channel, the cause, the source, then one can move through life from job to job, investment to investment, from business to business and stop wherever one is and commune with God and experience the fullness of that connection rather than just in certain buildings or certain places on earth. It's all good to know in truth that there is <u>no separation</u> from the Father/Mother who expresses all things and is the allness of all things. That only enhances all the goodness beyond comprehension.

Jesus on several occasions refers to our daily bread as the bread of life, our hidden manna. Jesus often made time for prayer and silence to still the mind and return to God's house. We are not designed to carry the burdens of our worldly experiences, but instead to give them to God, who knows what to do with them, freeing us up to do the work we really are meant to be doing, to focus on our dreams and goals, and to keep our side of the street clean. We need to nourish ourselves daily. It is how our souls receive the goodness and we can stay strong in alignment with life. Without it our pathway to our souls lives malnourished. And though the soul is always in a state of divine perfection, we need to do our part, for our minds will always be full, but of what? A body can feed until it's ready to burst but remain malnourished and so can the passage way to our souls.

Theorizing and psychoanalyzing are wonderful poetic words; but as beautiful and intellectual as they are, they will not fulfill us. They may comfort us for a week. It is in the realization that Divine Truth brought into demonstration guarantees wellness at work; work that begins with our thoughts being in alignment with our imagination. We are in the midst of absolute and perfect goodness, in infinite and eternal expression. Wisdom divine and perfect is here now in the eternal moment. We need not put our thoughts in the past or in the future. The infinite wisdom of all that is, right here, right now, and that is our daily bread.

Primitive being is still alive and well and living nice and snug amid the great technology and higher education of the twenty-first century. There is still a powerful need to rely heavily on denial.

This form of denial is nothing more than a primitive defensive reaction in dealing with living. There is a healthy form of denial such as denying illusions to influence the psyche. Often though, denial is used as that quick escape and it is quite habit-forming. The setback is a lack of faith and, as a result, not turning to the activity of God that is already in and of us. If we do not commune in God's Divine and beautifully perfect wisdom that we dwell in the midst of, we can only continue to fall prey to illusions. Even at their best, our illusions are so limiting compared to infinite and eternal wisdom.

Creation is designed in goodness. All that we need has already been given to us. When the Mother/Father finished with creating heaven and earth, the universal template was finished only because it was good. All complete, all providing, all nourishing in wisdom and grace and truth. In the beginning was the word…full of grace and truth.

Our soul accepts all our thoughts, often on a subconscious level. Then coinciding with the soul, our emotions produce the thought into form. Our soul is the way we work. We creatively process through our thoughts and in and of itself something will happen. We are spirit and that is where our thinking comes from. Soul is the way we work and in turn it is the happening we experience and respond to.

In truth we are the light. All of creation is the light in creation. So why fear the light? Why be attracted to darkness? We cannot run or hide from what all of creation is. The fear of goodness, its grace and wisdom, its love and wellness, its understanding and joy, is just what many are doing. Fear is always the culprit underlying all the disease and disharmony, all the unrest and gluttonous power.

It is all too easy to express from fear consciousness and become willing to consume and take from the earth rather than giving to the earth (the earth represents our outer state consciousness made manifest, collectively and individually). This only leads to living off a malnourished vibration. And if it becomes powerful enough, many become infected by these malnourished expressions. But when one awakens to the truth that we may be in the earth but we are not of it, then we begin to know harmony and abundance; we begin to understand true wealth and live in the riches of God's Kingdom. A kingdom that is here now, that we can find in wisdom. Wisdom is the seed of all that is. It is the energy and vibration of life. Whether we choose to work it wisely or not, it is always working in us as it is working in all things, for it is all things. We can construct or destruct. We can live in harmony and love or in hatred and agony. We can produce and multiply in grace, peace, and joy or we can crash and burn each step of the way. Know this, whatever we do, we do it to ourselves first. There is no way possible to not live off the vibration we produce.

A young man I know had a long run with drug addiction and had spent several times in jail. His life was deteriorating rapidly and all that he believed in had fallen by the wayside. Among his talents was songwriting. He had come to realize he was just a drug addict pretending to be a musician. What he loved dearly was nothing more than an illusion. His last time in jail became a blessing for him. He was able to not only get the drugs out of his system, but he had also begun to get them out of his mind. First he proclaimed to himself that he truly had enough of the way he'd been living. Then he came to believe that God had placed him there to "get his act together." His consciousness began to shift into the light and in doing so he began letting go of the false shadows that haunted him.

He has been back in society for a while now and has been in the studio recording his songs. His whole life has been devoted to a deeper understanding of these spiritual principles and he is in awe of how his life is proceeding. Those closest to him are joyfully surprised and even astounded with the way he is living and the life that he is building in God's Grace. Simply put, it works if you work it!

Our true vibration is of the universe divine. This is how we are built. The "we" meaning all of life. We are meant to have a reservoir of wisdom and knowledge, grace and peace, love and harmony, power and life pure and well in a complete order of balance.

This is the soul operating as it is meant to be. Only man pollutes, not God. Man can clean it up also, but not by man alone, but by man as one with the Divine Intelligence that is all present, all knowing, all powerful, all science. How can we possibly miss it? Denial and ego, as a team, can be very self-destructive. Like cannibals unto our own selves, we devour our being and sicken ourselves.

When we begin to nourish ourselves, the vibration of our souls make it clear what a beautiful universe we are a part of. We can play in God's playground with a creative freedom that jars the imagination in joy and glory, with plenty of room for everyone. Harmony cannot exist as one note but as many in creation to one joyful sound ringing out in the light of truth that is the light of everyone and everything. Our souls are meant to vibrate in a glory of harmonious wisdom and are an intricate part of who we are. It is part of our spiritual beings like the heart is to our physical bodies. It is what attunes us to this fantastic energy called life!

Lesson (Guidelines)
Prayer

I am life and there is no separation. Life is timeless and never ending, for life is creation itself. I am of the Divine Intelligence. I am of all creation. I dwell amid the splendor and beauty of Infinite Love. I am in the likeness, and all that is flows through me. I am a creative spirit expanding from absolute goodness. My imagination has purpose, and I have been given authority over my thoughts, ideas, and emotions. I have been given permission by Divine Life to create from love, wisdom, and grace. I am one with God and so it is. Amen *four*

Smile and Love

1 John 4:16
God is love. Whoever lives in love lives in God, and God in them.
1 John 4:19
We love because God first loved us.

Smile. Stop here for a moment and smile. You do not need a reason to smile for you are already connected, whether you feel it or not. So smile. Take a moment to clear your mind as best as possible and then smile. Be conscious of how your body is responding to the muscles in your face that are creating a smile. The whole body will shift to be in alignment to your smiling. Your mind is also your body, and though you may be in a space were you're not up for smiling, you still have authority to choose to do so even though emotionally you may not feel like it. Smile, just smile. Stick with this for a bit. Again, your mind is also part of your body and you have made the decision to smile. You have taken charge of your mind and now the mind has taken charge of the body.

Your mind will also reap the benefits of your decision. Take a couple of minutes, take several minutes, and allow your whole being to transform into a loving and caring vessel. First things first, love yourself. Don't wait for an outer world event to provide you with love. In doing so you are having trust and faith in the true source.

Why does this work? The answer is because God loves us first. It is in the nature of all creation, timeless and unchangeable. It is the reason why we have any clue at all of what is love. It is already in us. Love is energy. Love is absolute power in constant creation. It is undivided, whole, and infinite, eternal and pure, that which already is, the infinity of Alpha and the Omega.

The universe is in you as it is in everything, no more and no less. We cannot pray or ask for more; that prayer cannot be answered, for all that is already exists within all living things, fully and completely. From the largest galaxy to the smallest element, God is omnipresent. We can pray for realization of this truth. That prayer can be answered. We can pray to learn how to harness our consciousness into the tangible frequency of our Father/ Mother's infinite flowing stream of Divine Love and Wisdom. We can be a living witness to the Divine Truth. We can breathe in the pure Divine Expression of goodness and go forth and breathe out from it in a flowing, creative awareness of wellness in all we say and in all we do.

When I introduce to folks this simple notion to just smile, I see an immediate shift in the room's energy. Some folks give a bewildered smirk, others just immediately smile, some begin to laugh while keeping a smile upon their faces, and a few are moved to tears. The majority cannot resist, to one extent or another, smiling. This is a powerful healing practice. God's plan is perfect, there is a very good reason why we are capable of smiling, and we are empowered with the ability to do so simply because we choose to do so!

There is a blessing written over three thousand years ago found in the book of Numbers, 6:24–6, "The Lord bless you and keep you; The Lord make his face smile upon you, and be gracious unto you; the Lord lift his countenance upon thee, and give you peace." The Father/Mother of light is always expressing through us. We are the light in creation. We are the energy, and the substance of God is expressing through us, as us. God is life in creative expression, ever expanding in perfect motion.

As a child I remember hearing that God was everything, and I would walk along the pipelines and wooded areas thinking, "God is that rock and God is that tree and God is that sticker bush..."

That always stayed with me, but I had little to go on. Often it would haunt me because I had no idea about spiritual tools, let alone how to begin to use them.

God is everything and is everywhere. Within all elements is that cosmic and perfect wisdom in expression. As it turns out, that which would haunt me was only the universe calling to me; no matter how deep I tried to bury it into the depths of the darkest caverns of my mind, there was always that faint flicker of light. In truth, all the darkness in the world cannot hide even the smallest light, for in truth that is the illusion: that the darkness is deep and wide and the light is faint. It is the other way around. The light is the all of creation and the darkness is only the fear of the self-centered beast afraid to crawl out of its primordial ooze.

Whether it is a beautiful flower or a twisted up old piece of rusty metal lying in the bottom of a murky swamp, they are of the same elements.

We are perfect spiritual beings but the earthly ways fill us with limitation and fear. The true self is infinitely filled with Divine Wisdom, but we get really clogged up with the erroneous thoughts and the patterns of the race mind (self-will believing in separation). This though can always be unclogged. It comes down to what do I want to listen to? What do I want to absorb? What do I want to express?

What do I want to trust: television commercials and the nightly news, the sneering political innuendos of too many leaders trying to outdo each other with intellectual rudeness and sarcasm?

Or love? Divine Love is always there no matter what is going on or happening. When the winds of man's shadow have all been blown away, there will still be love. For love is how life is built and has created our being. Love is the wisdom of divine and infinite intelligence.

Love and spirit are perfect, but when love is filtered down, the little that is experienced can even become evil. Evil is defined as "being off one's true path," and relying on fear as a way to build a defense for surviving. Creating and building a lack of faith we end up depending too much upon stroking the ego with self-delusional concepts and thriving on egocentric illusions of space; callously utilizing ignorance as a means of accomplishment. Evil, defined and exposed as its true self, is ignorance. It is the pathway of erroneous thought brought into expression and made manifest.

We are perfect spiritual beings. This is the most important thing to remember: <u>we are perfect spiritual beings</u>. This is our minds' foundation, our place to start and build.

Fear is the disease that causes illness. Fear is the causation stemmed from the original sin; the original sin is in believing we live in separation. There is no separation, only one creative intelligence. The only true causation is God. Fear is the result of not believing in the Innate Intelligence.

Aperture science is the "first things first" of life transcended from the ether substance that is beyond thought and expressed as light, and that light is all wisdom in motion.

With forgiveness and nonblaming we realize and manifest the true self. God does not make junk, and God does not want anyone sick or suffering. God is love. God is wisdom. God is grace. God can only express love and grace and from that perfect action stems wisdom, peace, knowledge, power, joy, and life in alignment and therefore harmonious.

A friend of mine has had many challenges in her life that she has overcome with love. The positive mind that flows from this energy is the only power and encompasses all things, replenishing, nurturing, healing, and expanding. It is a realization that all has, after all, always been well.

At one point in her life she had a tumor in her breast. In her deep belief and faith, all she could see was love and not the tumor. Much to her doctors' astonishment, the tumor vanished as if it was never there. They had a hard time believing that she took no medication.

Another time in her life she had been in a car accident. She walked away with a minor injury, but that is not the story I wish to pass on. She immediately turned to God's love and peace and began seeing the goodness. She had to travel via the bus for a while and found great peace in her daily journeys commuting around locally. Though it meant leaving earlier, getting home later, and the bus was not always on time, she lived in the moment and saw the goodness and beauty. As it was, she had needed an additional car for one of her children. Within a reasonably short period of time from the accident came two cars. Some would call it luck or catching a break. But she was in the flow and goodness was what she vibrated out to the universe, and so it returned in goodness of abundance.

So let's make our way in the image of the Divine Wisdom that we are truly a part of, and just love ourselves, for we are beautifully and wonderfully made, and we come together because of the divine source. When we allow ourselves to be of this goodness, we then begin to realize we are this goodness. It is our nature. It is the law of attraction. When we allow ourselves to hinder our perfect selves, our beings become jaded and dulled and our minds become filled with distortion and errors causing a conflicting state of mind. The ways of the human race are insidious, placing endless veils over truth. The human psyche is so oversaturated and bombarded with lies and half-truths that when truth is present, it is twisted into being seen as the lie.

How do we see through this? With love. We begin to look at life with love. In doing so the shadows dissipate and the light vibrates resiliently, simply because the light was always there to begin with. Without it there is no life. Genesis 1:3, "And God said: 'Let there be light'; and there was light. And God saw the light, that it was good (good meaning complete in perfection).

It is in the love that we feel and that we then seek the light and become nourished. To love God with all our being is to love the true self. To love the true self is to love the allness of life. To have an understanding that is simple in nature but infinitely omnipotent and omniscient is to smile in the grace of life's energy and to drink from the fountain head of the inner knowledge of the Infinite Creative Intelligence (God). In the nature of Divine Intelligence, we need not force sight but only look with an inner eye. We need not words or thoughts. We need not contemplate or even concentrate. We need only in the silence of the word to be open-minded and receptive. Moving beyond the illusions of obliterated cadences, repetitiously saturating the world with contiguous shortcomings, one will see life alive and vibrant, abundant and full of grace.

It is when we live in love that we live in infinite harmony. When we have the gratitude to do this, we then realize the Father/Mother is in us. It is the only way we come to know and be of such great beauty, to embrace life and to truly breathe the breath of life. Suddenly there is no emptiness. There is only God in and through all divinity, as cosmic consciousness expels into deeper and deeper dimensions of all goodness and expresses in the loving harmony of the allness of I Am.

In this ether/spiritual water of light we grow to a higher state of consciousness; a super consciousness that is Christ Mind. Here the Spirit of Life generates God's Wisdom in a natural process of enlightening the birth energy, and it is here that we tap into and express into manifestation our revelations. We do so for we are in the image and likeness; we are God's children. It is our nature. It is our divine path of being and our inherent gift. It is in the absolute realization that it is the lamb (Christ Mind) that is the shepherd that guides the way, not the flesh. It is the blood of the lamb (Christ Mind/Consciousness) that runs through our spiritual vibration (the Holy Spirit), not the flesh. It is here we truly learn to surrender unto the cosmic soil that gives birth to that which grows in and of our innate Christ Mind.

And this all begins because we chose to smile, to have faith, knowing that faith is the activity of God's Divine goodness working in us as that perfect goodness works through all things. For the cosmic intelligence of perfect goodness is the allness of all things.

In my studio I have a painting by Doug Peden. It's called the *Cosmic Laugh*. At first glance you might see it as abstract but after you look at it for a while, you will realize that it is not abstract at all. In fact, it is a painting of a highly evolved mathematical expression creating rhythmic energy. It is musical. Each tone, color, and note gracefully compliments the other in an orchestra of graceful ripples. Deliberate patterns of GridField Geometry. It reminds me of the importance to smile. For in creation, first there is the smile, a smile that only comes from divine light. And from divine light there is deliberate purpose and perfection. And it is good!

When we become filled with the cosmic radiant light we will vibrate in an expression of wellness in the goodness of a perfectly designed universe.

So smile and love. We are the children of light; we do not belong in the darkness of our fears and doubts expressing extreme limitations. Often the illusion of our own making makes these fears and doubts look enticing. So we end up pulling from this limitation over and over again so that we might have a moment of indulging ourselves with temporary relief rather than expanding from that "cosmic smile."

We are so busy searching that we miss what is right at home. Omnipresence is everywhere, including right within the self, and the self is living in the midst of the Omnipresence. Searching for this is like going about sniffing our way around in hopes to find air, or like looking with sight to find our eyes.

Start to smile, and the smile will start the motion to love. It may need a jump start like a lawn mower getting cranked up for its first mow of the season. Sometimes you have to pull the chord a few times. If your faith is fading in and out, then just give it the benefit of the doubt. And give it your wholehearted attention. It gets very easy to put this on the back burner, slipping farther away, inch by inch, putting the outer world's current events first. We can get swept up in our own daily responsibilities and before long escape into them simply because of that inner disturbance that makes it uncomfortable to focus on our true divine nature. We continue to bury ourselves in our outer responsibilities, which look really good and even impressive. We might even get an award and have people cheer for us.

Smile and let that smile take you to a place where only something wonderful can happen. That something wonderful being love, a cosmic energy that was with you before you were even with you. This is the cosmic smile of all that is and has always been. There is a divine purpose for you—for you are of a perfect design of divinity, and you are love because you have always been loved. Know that your entire being is of that same goodness that is within all life. Let it radiate from you, knowing it's the same light within us all. To live in truth is to live in Love Divine.

So smile and love.

Lesson (Guidelines)
Meditation

Take a moment to pray in silence. When doing so smile.
Allow your whole being to become conscious of you smiling. Let every cell and fiber of your body become one with your smile.

Try not to have any thoughts, only awareness. Allow the smile to take its natural course.

If your smile increases, just let it do so.

Allow time to take its course. Do not interfere with it.

When the time has finished, gently return maintaining the smile. Open your eyes and look around. Again, try not to have any thoughts, only awareness. At the appropriate time, just say thank you and proclaim that all is well.

In this meditation you have trusted in the Holy Spirit to guide you in Christ Mind.

And so it is. God bless.

five
Where Is Now?

1John: 2:15-16
Love not the world, neither the things that are in the world. If
any man love the world, the love of the Father is not in him.
For all that is, in the world, the lust of the flesh, and the lust of the
eyes, and the pride of life, is not of the Father, but is of the world.

Revelation 1:11
I am the Alpha and the Omega, the first and the last...

Matthew 6:33
Seek ye first the kingdom of God, and his righteous-
ness: and all these things shall be added unto you.

Wisdom is God Science expressing in light, and its energy vibrates life perfectly and lovingly as one. We are the wisdom, light, and energy of the Mother/Father's perfect expression. In this Divine Truth, there is only the motion of the eternal moment. We can turn to it always, wherever and whenever. That is why we do not wait on life. We only end up waiting on ourselves to show up. Life is eternal and timeless. Life is now. We can daydream about tomorrow or reflect on yesterday, but we only live in the moment.

When we learn to surrender and to allow ourselves to be conscious of the infinite current of life flowing through us in energy so fantastic, we can begin in the awareness that we shape life here on earth rather than be pulled around by the sum expression that has already manifested on the ever changing earth. The ways of society are only there because humankind has shaped them so. We can be completely influenced by them, never questioning them and letting them direct us and help us. On the other hand, we are not God. When I say we are not God, I mean we are not the energy source. We are not the fountainhead of inner knowledge. We are of the Creator and we are creative beings; in spirit we are perfection, in the flesh we are a constant variety of hit and miss. Living out of balance and too much in the flesh it becomes all too easy to believe and devote ourselves to journeys that we really never needed to be on, having manipulated ourselves into believing it was really important to leave the Garden of Eden and go into the land of *Nod.

*Self-will, when not living in erroneous thought, functions from the core of God's Being and can creatively express God's Wisdom as an individual expression. When living in the illusion of time as a limited space from which to function, self-will dominates from its own self-centeredness and creates with an extremely limited capacity, simply because we're not "tapped in." An example would be the reason why we still have wars and use brute force both physically and psychologically as a means to acquire power for self-indulgences. It is extremely primitive and childish on a barbaric level.

At first when one becomes aware of this, usually there is a rebellious reaction that brings forth resentment, anger, vengeance, and depression. Continuing to stay in it is to be but a mirror that continues to take the bait by counter acting. At best one is covering new shadows and veils over the old shadows and veils.

We are so much more than that. We can live and create in the expression of the laws of truth. As mentioned earlier, don't just pray for something; begin to live as if you've already received. We need not live in fear as we walk in the valley of the shadows of negative thoughts; we need only walk as children of light. For the light is all powerful and the *all* of everything. The light is love energy vibrating a passageway of being.

It is the harmonious breath of true purpose and the divine order of creative expression. It fills and lifts consciousness beyond the outskirts of the abstract beginning, allowing us to extrapolate into a perfect and beautiful understanding of God Idea, complete and fulfilling. It brings clarity to the mind, allowing us to see that the kingdom is here, now. All we need to do is be receptive and willing to receive. But to be receptive one must see, and we have placed so many veils over our own eyes and clouded our own passage way with trinkets and glitter that it takes a good jolt just to crack the cosmic debris and let some light in. The tragedy is to live so deep in the race mind and to be filled with so much erroneous thought that when truth is present it is perceived as the lie. Yet all we need is to be conscious of this moment right here. To still the mind, right now. After all, if not now then when? The moment is ours to be receptive to truth right now! Contemplate, concentrate, and meditate on it. The true inner self wants the truth.

If it scares you, let it. If it makes you feel uneasy, let it. We can begin a journey of truth or throw another veil over it. That has been the ongoing solution for many generations since the beginning of time. And that gets passed on to each generation. When the Bible states that we inherit our ancestors' sins, this is what it means. We're not doomed to this. We can let go of it and surrender it over to the cosmic consciousness of Father/Mother/ God. We need not wait. The moment is now. When we are ready, God is already there. Humankind has been fighting God's battles instead of surrendering them over so that we may be free to learn from God's Wisdom, Kingdom, Grace, Love, and Peace; to begin to enter into an understanding of nonblaming. To live in a state of nonblaming is to move beyond forgiving. We do not need to forgive if we are living in a consciousness of nonblaming.

The greatest gift is that we have consciousness. We can take it to a divine level rather than just a reaction that enslaves us to the daily conditions of happenchance and manipulated concepts about life. We choose how we wish to feel about anything and everything right down to our most personal beliefs.

We allow the outer world's conditions to shape our moods. It is our decision to go where we wish to go with it. We have dominion over our thoughts, ideas, emotions, and imaginations.

Our physical self is but only a shadow garment expressing our state of mind. That holds true for all of life. First there is consciousness, then there is thought.

When we become conscious of the science of God's Wisdom, we then begin to live in truth. Suddenly a lot of the important things begin to look childish and unimportant. The tomorrows and yesterdays, and even the todays begin to have an illusion about them. We can only live in the eternal moment. We begin to claim the self, listening to the true heart pursuing the things that really matter to us rather than what we've been told to follow. We begin to realize there is purpose, there is life and it's ours. We begin to show up for our lives.

We make manifest what is within our cosmic dreams. They are ours to shape, to mold, to live in vibrant dimensions of oneness, endless and fulfilling. It is our innate imagination, infinite and ever expanding.

More and more in my life I see it going the way my imagination sees it. Often in the past I settled for what society called the "right thing to do." I did that over and over and there would be moments where I felt good about what I was doing, but there was always an emptiness inside that would catch up with me and run me over. It wasn't until I came to know that the prayer that never fails is simply, "Seek ye first the kingdom of God, and his righteousness: and all these things shall be added unto you," Matthew 6:33.

This is the great law that Jesus awakened us to. Within it is the law of mind, the law of forgiveness, the law of expression, and the law of attraction. To seek the kingdom of God is to expand in Christ Mind; to expand in Christ Mind is to have a deeper understanding of the kingdom of God.

Recently, in the simplicity of life, I had a gift from the most high. My work that I do in a correctional center with the men and women is a blessing for me. I have been doing positive affirmations of "I am." Example: I am good, I am peace, I am love, I am creative, etc. The men and women have been very receptive to it. I yell it out loud and they yell it back.

One morning I had forgotten my ID card, which I never do. I had to go to the lobby to get a pass. As they were making me the pass card, I heard two women's voices yelling out, "I am beautiful. I am love!"
I turned to see two of the women I had been working with. They had been released and were on their way home. One ran up to me and hugged me and yelled out, "And I am free!!!" I reminded them of the power of positive mind and to keep believing in the positive "I am," and to stay far away from the negative "I am." To keep discovering and unfolding in their true innate nature.
The natural flow has nothing to do with coincidences. My forgetting my ID was part of the plan that morning. Today I see this with eyes to see and ears to hear. These things are happening all the time. Often we blindly miss them. Today I do not and I rejoice in them. This is a big part of living in the now! In fact, on that same day, when I got to my desk, the assistant director asked me if I would like to start a new group called "Who Am I?" Coincidence? Not at all! So I say to you, arise with eyes open and ears to hear. Rejoice and believe!

We begin to live by the sacred Kingdom of Knowledge, a knowledge that has no boundaries, where there is no good or evil or life or death. We move beyond a world of duality and realize there is only good. God's good. When we begin to go beyond the outskirts of infinity, we see that there is only being; there is no separation, only creative expression. It is then that we have begun to stop living in the noise. We begin to stop falling prey to its cunning disguises, often our own voices sounding off and manipulating and deflating our psyches and filling them with well-defined misconceptions that keep us, so-called, safe and sound. All the while we are falling into this extremely limited state, and our minds are racing everywhere, except being conscious of the moment—the only moment we live in. The rest are thoughts drifting all over, going in and out of each other. To stop and seize the moment is to vibrantly grasp truth and ride it into fruitful expression. This is our dominion to take charge of.

Now is where we deliver our creativity into becoming a part of life. Now is where we live and feed the vibration that we express from. Now is where goals are brought into success. Now is the time for showing up and living. Now is where we are in true consciousness. Now is where only the eternal moment lives in infinity. Now is where we are truly doing what it is we are doing.

Now is love. Now is the wisdom that we breathe into our souls and fill our hearts with Divine Harmony Supreme.

The errors of the ways of the world leave us for they cannot live in this glorious moment. It is so easy to fall prey to a burned-out state of mind and a broken heart, and to be drastically overwhelmed. It can pull us into a false abyss of sadness and depression. That is where the world lives without faith and without the wisdom that fulfills us. God's omnipresent, omniscient, and omnipotent activity never stops working in us. It is here, now, in this moment. Wake up to it and take off from it. Bring God's Kingdom into everything you do. Demonstrate it with every step and every breath you take, for it is in the moment, right here, right now. You don't have to wait for it. It's the other way around. It has been waiting for you. Rejoice in it. Love in it. Laugh in it. Live well in it!

We need not tarry in pride nor trudge in self-centered illusions of victorious moments. We can move to higher ground and live as a child of the Light of Life.

It is our Father/Mother who art in heaven that gives us the awakened mind of light and purpose. We have this wonderful and astounding ability to be witnesses to life, to be a part of it, to thrive from it and in it, to exuberantly soar beyond our beliefs, and to bask in the glory of God Consciousness.

In the beginning was the word and the word was grace and truth, and the word was made flesh. Life was breathed into our nostrils and we became the I am of I Am. We are the expression of life itself always being. There is only this moment. Now is here. You are in I Am. We are in I Am. The past, the present, and the future is I Am.

Live in the present moment and live in the presence of our all-perfect Cosmic Parent. There is nowhere else. Your ideas are the ideas of life and your victories are the nervous system of the universe. Feed it well. Nourish it with the heavenly kingdom. Poison it and live among the dead who just beat themselves over and over again in a progressive continuum of negativity. To live in the eternal moment of truth is to live in a never-ending cup that runneth over in abundant love, peace, and harmonious creativity. It is the law of expression as one with the law of attraction.

Allow yourself to be witness to this beautiful and perfectly designed eternal moment. Where there is divine principle involved, there is no need to ascertain the facts, running this way or that way hoping to gather them up.

Welcome to your life; you are here. "Now" is where you have always been. Open your mind and watch it soar beyond the galaxies of your deepest imagination.

You are a child of the Light of Life. You are God's child. Blessed and filled with the holy kingdom just waiting for you to make manifest in Christ Mind. Use the tools in the goodness of life and watch the flowing well-being of your consciousness make manifest. The tools are the same stuff you are made of: peace, knowledge, understanding, wisdom, power, joy, and life. They are our inherencies from God. They are the oneness of cosmic intelligence: the Mother, the Father, God. To use them is to be one with the kingdom, to feed from the endless fountain of creation itself.

Live in the moment. Live now. This is where you are: complete and perfect in the perfect eternal cosmic light, a spirit child. One with your Creator, and therefore one with all of life.

*Cain went away from the presence of the Lord and settled in the land of Nod, east of Eden" (Genesis 4:16). Cain settling "east of Eden" implies that he was farther removed from the garden than Adam and Eve were. He was to live as an outsider.
Nod, in Hebrew, means "wanderer, exile, or fugitive." He would be a fugitive and a wanderer on the earth (Genesis 4:12). Metaphysically, Nod is not an actual place; rather, it is a state of being; wherever Cain went, it could be called the "land of the Wanderer."
Though God had driven Cain from his home, it was only because of Cain's choice to live outside the presence of God. Cain, in becoming a wanderer and a fugitive, would lose all sense of belonging and identification. Living in the "land of Nod," Cain was disconnected, thrusting himself into sin. Cain was a castaway and godless; a hollow person in the land/consciousness of Nod. Cain built a society totally detached from God. The Bible tells us that his children followed in his path and made manifest a godless civilization (Genesis 4:16–24).

Lesson (Guidelines)

Take the time throughout the day to stop and become aware of "the moment." Become conscious of your body and life around you. Ask yourself these questions. (*You may want to copy these questions onto a card so that you may have them with you at all times.*)

- Are your thoughts really centered into the divine moment?
- How often are you drawing conclusions to things that are yet to happen or may never happen?
- Are you rehashing the past and not letting go, and in turn not moving on?
- Are you letting someone else's poor behavior get to you?
- If so, how is this helping you mentally and emotionally?
- Are you taking time to include prayer and meditation?
- If so, are you comfortable with how much time you spend in prayer and meditation?
- Are you often placing your mind into thoughts of turmoil?
- Are you willing to surrender it all over to a Higher Power of divine goodness and wisdom?
- Are you ready to tap into and receive this absolute goodness into your life and become willing to do what it takes to start practicing it?

Take the time now to review the guidelines at the end of the previous chapters. Let them into your life. Give thanks to the Omnipresent, Omniscient, Omnipotent Light of Life. Rejoice and believe!!

Peace

six

Part One: That Fiery Inferno, That Bottomless Pit...The Subconscious
Part Two: Four Laws of Living in Fantastic Energy

Revelation 9:2–3
And he opened the bottomless pit; and there arose a smoke out of the pit, as the smoke of a great furnace; and the sun and the air were darkened by reason of the smoke of the pit. And there came out of the smoke locusts upon the earth; and unto them were given power...

Part One

We are searching for peace, happiness and joy, often in all the wrong places. After a while it begins to catch up with us. We have buried unfinished business and same thought patterns with new outer makeup, such as friends, cars, homes, jobs, locations, drugs (prescribed or not prescribed), etc.

Finding happiness once again slips through the fingers as just another illusion. The subconscious, the bottomless pit, smolders in all its unfinished and confusing experiences, discoloring our demeanor with deep buried regrets, resentments, moods, unfinished business, and attitudes that show up in the disguise of "no rhyme or reason," leaving only pain, suffering, and bitterness.

Desperation of frantically consuming the material/outer world, looking for release, creates an insatiable appetite that is never quite fulfilled. The line from the Lord's Prayer, "On earth as it is in heaven," is often ignored. At best, an occasional thanks to God and then for the moment God is okay.

In this state of ungrace, what do we have to compare to in regards to our experiences, especially on an emotional level? We call it the nature of things. It's in my blood, it's part of my heritage or cultural beliefs. We are so much more than just beasts forever trying to climb out of that primordial ooze. Clawing and scraping at one another just for that next latest fad.

We are spirit. And we are made in divine perfect order. We are in our Creator's image and therefore have free will. That is where we need to take responsibility of such a priceless gift and learn to function from what we are truly made of: God's Wisdom and grace. It flows through us; it is us. Its words whisper in every fiber of our being. This is where we learn the meaning of joy. It can only be found within. Joy changes the entire meaning of our purpose. It is in the spiritual experience of joy that we take charge of the subconscious and douse the raging fire from the smoldering bottomless pit. It is then that we stop spewing out the locusts and scorpions of our negative, depressed state. Now we have a foundation to build upon. A foundation built on rock not sand, mud, and whirlpools.

We move beyond the animalistic predatory response. We begin to stop being part of that psyche that feeds off of one another's fears and doubts, which is a give and take sharing of endless crises and taking sides for emotional nourishment in the battle to win to fight another day.

It's the nature of things that comes from living in duality. There is no separation in God Mind. There is only one power, all good. It's not about right or wrong or good and bad. Do we just inhale and not exhale? We are of the One. The One being only of love, peace, grace, knowledge, wisdom, understanding, and joy.

When one begins to see with his or her eyes open, to truly see life, one's whole expression changes as does the attraction. When we let go of the blaming, criticizing, resentments, and bitterness, stop going around with a chip on the shoulder and condemning, then we have cleared the self-made wreckage and now we can see what is truly there. Divine Goodness right at our fingertips, waiting for us to partake in all that it is here on earth, right now in this moment as it is in heaven. Stop the censuring and begin with His Kingdom already within you. Do not allow the locusts and scorpions to continue to germinate in your subconscious. You have dominion.

There is a story of two monks who were walking along a road that was very muddy. There had been torrential rains earlier, and now they were making their way as best as possible. After a while they came across a young attractive woman who was desperately trying to cross the road with no success. Their vows did not allow them to have conversation with people; even between themselves there was very limited talk, unless otherwise moved by the Holy Spirit. The one monk broke away from the other and went over to the woman and offered her his assistance. He picked her up and carried her to the other side of the road and gracefully let her down, and then went on his way with the other monk. In addition to not allowing conversation, the monks' vows discouraged the touching of women. The other monk was enraged and furious with the one who helped out the young woman. Early that evening they stopped to rest and eat. The monk who had helped the woman earlier that day said the other monk, "You seemed agitated all day and still so. Are you upset with me?" The other monk replied, "Yes, I am very upset with you! You went over to that woman, spoke to her, and then picked her up and carried her across the muddy road! Do you not know our vows?" He replied, "Yes I do brother. I did talk with her. I did pick her up and carried her across the muddy road and then I let her go, and that was the end of it. But you, on the other hand, have not let her go and are still carrying on about it." With that said, they both had a good laugh and continued on with their journey.

Come face-to-face with the smoldering anger, resentments, and suffering that have been festering for way too long and see them for what they are: damaging to the core of your happiness. They do not have a mind of their own. They belong to you and you can get rid of them all. They have no power other than the power you allow them to have.

Understanding is not enough. Once we have an emotional attachment to our thoughts it becomes hard to let go. And though it may be hard, it is not at all impossible. There are laws/principles at work here. In this chapter I would like to focus and center in on four of them. We have been looking at them thus far to a certain degree. The four laws are vital in their order and the ability to move on in the grace of goodness.

These four laws are: the law of surrender, the law of mind, the law of expression, and the law of attraction.

Part Two

The Law of Surrender

> *Nehemiah 8:10*
> *"The joy of the Lord is your strength."*

The first law is the law of surrender. It is here that we forgive and can restore ourselves by freeing ourselves from the collected experiences brought on by the race mind. On any given day, in any given moment, we absorb all that is around us. Often we can get caught up in the daily hustle and bustle without even leaving our homes, or, for that matter, even while on vacation. There is a lot of supported negative information out there and now it's infested into one's thought patterns; and if not already it is most definitely on the verge of expressing with the sole purpose of making manifest.

The immediate reaction is to retaliate, to defend, and/or to stand one's ground either by confrontation or by calling a friend with a sympathetic ear or to just try to bury it somewhere deep inside; perhaps to turn to God and complain about it.

The sooner we begin to forgive, the sooner we can let go and see the light of truth. These daily man-made shadows have no true power. As emotionally and even as physically painful as they may be, vengeance only claims them the winner. For now we have inherited their consciousness. A consciousness built only on empty illusions and erroneous thought now deep in our psyche.

Faith is the knowing that the activity of Divine Intelligence is already at work in us, completely, perfectly—infinitely. If that is not something you can accept, then try just giving it the benefit of the doubt; but not just a little bit, truly give it that benefit with all your heart. Be a witness unto your own self.

It is here that this law must come into play first. It is the foundation of the four laws. They must come into alignment within themselves. One is the other and, in fact, they are all of the same cosmic breath. We break it down so that we can comprehend on a deeper awareness. As this practice becomes a way of functioning, we need less and less to see this inseparable division because we are living in truth.

It is our Mother/Father who takes on our battles. We are not here to live our lives entangled in endless self-centered battles. As we surrender them over to the Universe of Life, we surrender the self-trapped egocentric convictions over to the One who truly knows how to deal with such matters. These fights do not belong to us, they belong to our Creator. It is not our job to play God but to be Godly in the image, to begin to grow up and out as we leave the root and begin our journey to the crown.

We can surrender into the protection of Divine Life all good and find forgiveness onto others and ourselves. We can then become restored and the second law can function in a healthy and harmonious experience.

It does not matter how often we return to be restored. As often as need be is the key ingredient. Let it become a beautiful habit. To not do so is the only tragedy.

Law of Surrender Prayer
Man's world and man's achievements are neither bad nor good. Free me from that thought of duality. There is only one power all good, all wise, all loving, and full of grace and peace. I cleanse myself in your truth and I am restored. Life is eternal and infinite. The dimensions are infinite and my journey is a recurring metamorphous of becoming whole and complete. The expressed manifestation from the root of man is not my place. My place is here in the eternal moment on earth as it is in heaven. I free myself from the erroneous thoughts whether they bind me or do not bind me at this time. I seek clarity. I seek the wisdom of science eternal, full of love divine and supreme.

I hold this truth in my heart to nourish my soul so that I may go forth on this vibration of truth.
And so it is!

The Law of Mind

> James 1:8
> "A double-minded man is unstable in all his ways."
> John 8:32
> "Ye shall know the truth and truth shall set you free."

The design of the universe is the template and road map for us to experience and grow. We are in the likeness, and the Creator lives and breathes all of life. All of creation is of the One and all is the expression of Cosmic Mind. Wisdom is the seed of birth. We are thinkers and that thinking is spirit, the experience of our thinking is soul. We are spirit and the soul is how we work. We live off the soul's process of vibrating our thoughts, generating emotional patterns and producing them into form.

Herein lies the true power. Praying to God to shift the axis of the universe to suit our needs is an endless and unanswered prayer. God just is and I am. That's it.

Trying to bend, change, and manipulate the universe with petitions is to live in race mind: believing in God perhaps, having faith perhaps, following God perhaps.

We are not meant to follow; we are to know the truth: that we are one with God Omnipresent, Omnificent, Omnipotent. We are in and of the allness of His/Her being.

These four laws cannot be altered. The law of mind will mirror what you feed it. It will make manifest. All that Divine Intelligence dwells within us, not in dribs and drabs divided up to the ones with the most gold stars for being very good. There is no division. The allness of our Creator is complete in each and every living thing. His/Her Wisdom is the spark; the light that ignites and forms all living things. Truth is already with us. We filter it. We mix it into our lack of understanding and even into no understanding.

It's not about right or wrong or good or bad. There is no duality. There is our expression. This is why the law of surrender is best dealt with first so as we become conscious of the law of mind. We now have dominion and can work with it as it is intended for us to work with it. We can feed the soul healthy soul food rather than bland, destructive, or flat-out rotten soul food. We can feed our souls the food we want to feed it rather than someone else's leftovers.

God gave us our individualism in the infinite and eternal oneness. We need not succumb to whatever are the latest fad, cultural event, peer pressure, stinking thinking, sounds, noise, guilt trips, being the hippest, family secrets, and even religion. We don't have to be dragged up and down the street just because that's what's going on today. These things end. And when they end, nobody really cares anymore because there's a whole new array of man's opinions and styles to engulf ourselves in.

We can choose wisely what we wish to be a part of and what we like to enjoy.

The law of mind just is and it is principle. When we put principle before personality, we put our entire being into alignment with Divine Mind.

The law of mind is ours to work with, to partner up with, and to live beautifully with in the midst of Infinite and Divine Intelligence. Christ Mind is within us all, and we can raise our consciousness beyond measure; beyond the outskirts of infinity. We are of One Mind, all good, all wise, all love; the endless, timeless Alpha and Omega.

Law of Mind Prayer
I am restored and my mind is at ease, freed from worries and doubts. My heart is filled with thankfulness and gratitude. I come before you humbled. I am no longer trapped in the ego state of race mind. I turn the problems of the world over to you as I turn my personal concerns and my fears and resentments over to you. I am a reflection of your goodness and love. My mind is cleansed and open and receptive to your goodness. I allow your love to be my love, your peace to become my peace, your wisdom to become my wisdom, and your wellness to become my wellness. I am open-minded and receptive to the Cosmic Truth and I am ready, completely ready to receive, to live, to trust, to believe with my entire mind, my heart, and my soul, with all my strength in a thanksgiving of forgiveness. As I bless my entire being, I bless all of creation.
Amen.

The Law of Expression

Hebrews 11:6
"*For he that cometh to God must believe that He is, and that He is a rewarder of them that diligently seek him.*"

1 Corinthians 2:12
"*Now we have received, not the spirit of the world, but the spirit which is of God: that we might know the things that are freely given to us of God.*"

God is I AM and God is as I am. To live in this consciousness is to express in this consciousness. To express in this consciousness is to demonstrate the activity of God already working in and through us. It is to know truth and live in its Divine Wisdom.

Bringing the law of surrender and the law of mind into alignment we can now see the Fruit of Life as it really moves and lives. As we demonstrate this action there is clarity. We can feel ourselves in the world but not of it, as if man's dimension and/or psyche have been removed from us.

We see we really are not a part of it and do not need its mountains and mountains of confusing remedies, its ill-gotten solutions, and problems to solve problems. For every cause there is an effect. Man is constantly focused on the effects created by the ego self, but rarely looks at the cause. In truth the only causation is God. There are those who like to dress up and manipulate the effect, creating illusions upon illusions, and leave their signature on it for all to see. Though it looks spectacular, it can not even begin to match the true causation that is already within you. The Christ substance waiting for you to make manifest in God's glory.

When we allow ourselves to express from the fountainhead of life's supreme inner knowledge and become enlightened in it and allow the inner knowledge to illuminate us in the light of Christ Consciousness, we are removed from the limitations of generations of illusions and erroneous thought; the shadows are cast down to nothingness and we soar in the light of infinite current. We discover and explore, we expand and rejoice, and we give thanks and dwell in the abundance of God's all good nature.

The law of expression is the *everything* we need. It has been available since creation itself for us to have and mold, to create and breathe. It is God's playground and we are all invited. What many need is to see is that we all are already in the playground; so please, start playing.

These laws, will mirror what we want consciously or unconsciously. It is our power. We can use it blindly and foolishly. One can cause harm unto themselves and others by having no faith and dwelling in misery.

Start feeding the soul good healthy soul food and work these beautiful laws in God Mind. Trust the heavenly Father/Mother. You are a divine child of the utmost good. These Laws are gifts for us all to work in harmonious love.

Law of Expression Prayer
Thank you! It is in this knowing that I do not ask for anything and I only hold truth in light. Be it a friend or a loved one who is troubled, I hold them in your light. I see only wellness and good, peace and grace, wisdom and love, knowledge and understanding, and I rejoice in you. Thank you. All I need is thee and all is well.
I remain diligent and steadfast in your being, infinite, all good, all supreme, all power.
I now take the time to contemplate briefly the statement, "Be still and know that I am God." And I now sit in your silence in your peace as I pray without words or thought.
And so it is.
Amen.

The Law of Attraction

1 John 4:4
"Greater is he that is in you, than he that is in the world."

2 Corinthians 9:11
"Being enriched in everything to all bountifulness,
which causeth through us thanksgiving to God."

The fourth law now falls into place. We are open to the truth and we are receptive to it. Though the law of attraction falls into place, we must be willing to receive it. If this is not occurring then it is best to double-check; a spot check, if you will. Search the heart and soul through contemplation, meditation, and discuss with like-minded folks. Perhaps the idea or a part of it is still in the mind and has not quite made it to the heart and soul. Live your prayer in a state of mind knowing you have already received the answer; an answer that is filled with peace and joy. Do not look to the world but within. Let it guide you and allow the true expression of your wellness to make manifest. Sometimes our dreams can get in the way. We visualize what we think is the answer, or think the answer is in a certain individual. Envisioning the answer can be very limiting and very draining. Trust your conscious being. If you are living in peace and joy then you're living in harmony with life. Allow that energy to guide you.

When we have aligned ourselves by surrendering through forgiveness and by cleansing the mind of race mind negativity, and when we have put Christ Mind at the helm of our consciousness allowing God Activity to flow and express through us, we then are right with all of creation.

The magnets of the shadows cannot attach to us. We see they are not truth and are not real. Their illusions can only be expressed in that consciousness.

They are not of Divine Mind and Divine Mind does not even see them because they are of the nothingness. Choosing to live in the false belief of separation is the only evil that prevails. It is the essence of the original sin. To live in separation is to live in ignorance and ignorance is sin. It goes forth misguided and then creates solutions to lessen the severity of living in separation but not to leave it. Instead, choosing to feed what is needed to stay on that course, going deeper and deeper down the river of denial and conjuring up new and brilliant ways to dwell and survive in the ignorance of living in separation.

When we truly live and demonstrate the law of expression, the law of attraction falls into place. We can walk through the valley of the shadows of erroneous thoughts and not be infected by it. It will not be attracted to us; it cannot really see us. At best it may be confused by us, but when it sees we won't play the game it becomes bored and dissipates.

You are running on God Power not man's idea of power. It may seem even a little strange to you at first and at times. It's okay. Give the mind time to adjust. Allow time for your mind to comprehend. All is good and all is well. Let Go and trust the goodness. We don't need the old defense systems any more.

We are spirit our temple is mammal. We have authority over it and in all we express here on earth. First there is consciousness, then thought, and then ideas put into creative motion to make manifest of the idea.

Let go and surrender the race minds extreme limitation over to the compassion of the innate self as one with the Mother/Father and take charge of your destiny. It is yours to create, unfold, and expand, soaring to places never dreamed of. Boldly make thunder and sound your trumpet in His/Her name and make manifest the glory of the Divine Beauty of the perfect Infinite Love Supreme.

Choose wisely, for wisdom is a science. It is the science of the omnipresent, all-perfect, all-loving Father/Mother of light and life for you are in it and of it. Make it so!

Prayer for the Four Laws

I am awakened by your breath of life. I am alive and I am a witness to your perfect goodness and beauty. Help me to stay on course, and when I falter may I be conscious and receptive to your lifting me back up into state of grace. Through your strength and your love I now know I can go deeper and deeper into my God Being and practice these four laws with the dedication and discipline of love and grace. Peace is the essence and well-being to this beautiful awareness, for it is truth. Your truth, your gift. I am blessed and eternally grateful. I humbly go forth as a being of peace and love in Christ Consciousness. I am under your care and your guidance. My cup runneth over in your wellness, and I am in harmony with all that you are and in all that you have created and will create. I know that you have always loved me and I am now in that love, feeling it flow

through the entire being of all that I am. For the Christ in me is the Spirit Substance and the Spirit Life.
Amen and amen.

Practice

It is important to remember that all of this is a practice. It's all about progress not perfection.

Review these four laws. Let them become a part of your heart and soul. Pick one of the prayers, in their order, each day and spend time in contemplation and meditation with them.

Trust the inner innate voice to guide you, allowing the wisdom of the Spirit of Life/Holy Spirit to fill you with the joy of truth.

In trusting your innate self you may not read all of it. You will stop where you need to stop to contemplate or meditate on a certain sentence or paragraph.
You may move on and continue reading or you may be finished.

In this practice you will, after a while, become acutely aware of your innate mind guiding you.

Peace and Blessings.

seven

One Creative Thought: I Am

I Corinthians 2:12
We have not received the spirit of the world but the Spirit who is from God, that we may understand what God has freely given us.

John 14:16-17
And I will ask the Father, and He will give you another Counselor to be with you forever—The Spirit of Truth. The world cannot accept him, because it neither sees him nor knows him. But you know him, for he lives with you and will be in you.

I once heard a sermon on the three ways of praying. The first one is of little faith, commonly nicked name the "foxhole prayer." It involves begging and pleading, demanding and insisting on what one wants rather than asking, "What do you want of me?" The person who prays in this manner is of the mindset that the world has done them wrong and that God hasn't the time for them. He's just too busy with more important matters and has no time for my insignificant suffering. This person insists that his will be done rather than God's will be done.

I cannot stress enough that we are in the image and likeness, and like begets like. In some places God is called Father in others Mother. Why is that? Does a mother and father abandon or not care for the their children? Do they not place them first before all things? Does not the mother and father want to care for, protect, teach, and love their children? Do not look to the illusions for the answer. In the outer world of our expressed ideas made manifest, some people who would call themselves mother or father have not been that at all. They may have had children but never earned the right to be called parents. So, let me say again do not look to the outer world of our expressed ideas made manifest. That is not where the answer dwells. That is only the sum of our ideas. Look within to your heart, your innate instinctive self. Do not compare God to us. Instead look to see our divine and beautiful purposeful potential. We are love, and in that love is grace, wisdom, compassion, knowledge, strength, and joy. We stem from the Omnipresence of God as one. God's love is our love and that love is the power and energy that moves wisdom into harmony.

There is no separation. All is one. So this first prayer can leave a person trapped in erroneous thought simply because they have put this thinking into manifestation and, as mentioned in the law of mind, it will mirror one's conscious state of being.

In the second form of prayer, the person has the type of faith where they truly believe in God and tries to follow the teachings. At the same time, the person confuses being humble with self-loathing and still feels that they are not important to the plans of God. God is out there somewhere and maybe, just maybe, if they are good enough, God just might hear and grant the prayer. A devout follower but does not believe or is not aware that we live in the midst of God, within and without. God is the allness of everything and that wisdom breathes life into all that exists. For life is God's Creative Wisdom.

The third way of praying simply says, "Thank you. Amen." This one knows all that is has already been and is at work in the eternal moment of life. We need to know this with all our mind, body, heart, and soul so that we may live in it and practice it. It's all about knowing that all is well for the Divine Mind is perfect in goodness, perfect in love and peace, and perfect in grace and wellness. We need not know our future. If we believe all is well then the journey is all we need. For the journey is a journey of wellness and peace ever unfolding from itself.

I Am that I Am was the name given to Moses when he asked, "Who are you?"

I Am that I Am: Omnipresent, Omniscient, Omnipotent, and All Perfect. We are perfect creations in search of perfection. Not the self-centered perfect or the narcissistic perfect or even the outer world achievement perfect. None of the illusions disguised as perfect. Spiritual breath perfect. I Am that I Am and all is good. As Divine Mind breathed life into the void, Divine Mind breathed the Spirit of Holy Spirit/Mediator into our consciousness and we were awakened to know, to see, to be a witness—to rejoice in life. God Truth flowing through our life being, gently whispering in its infinite power, "I am your song, your water, your food, your love. I am always with you…I will never forsake you."

Be still and listen to that voice that is of you but not of the world. That spirit of inner knowledge of God Mind, already knowing and passing on, is more a part of you than your own flesh. All that God is, is closer to you than you'll ever be onto your own self. We have the passion and the divine purpose to rise up in consciousness and expand within the infinite beauty and dwell in ceaseless prayer. The harmonious journey into the self, the image, to be in Christ Mind and love as our Mother/Father loves, returns us to the Eden Consciousness that has always been. We have buried it in erroneous thoughts and discolored illusions.

The world is an expression of our collaborated thoughts and ideas, and God's world is the absolute goodness of infinite creation. We cannot live consciously in both simultaneously. We can hop around from one to the other for a while. The attraction of each sways us back and forth. This is what we call the tree of life and the tree of the knowledge of good and evil.

God's knowledge and wisdom will guide us and our breaths will be the Creator's and our experiences will hear the universe calling and supplying us with what we need as we go forth in living and loving life. Why? For it always was there in the first place. To not know this is a tragedy of great suffering.

Do not let fear fill you with doubt. Just look around you. Look with awe and surrender. See the vast unbelievable activity of creation at work. Put aside the "me-isms"; see the universe and listen to it, for it is calling. It speaks in a language of the spirit, your spirit, for it is you, there is no separation. The knowing, the guiding is already at work in you. Listen to it. It's love supreme, all wise, all compassion, all wellness, at work, right now, in you.

I cannot stress enough the power of I am and what you place after these two words. In oneness we hear God is I Am, but we also hear, God is I am.

We are one. Taking God's name in vain is to place a negative statement after I am. God is not those negative, demeaning words, so they can only produce low self-esteem, low self-worth, even illness, disease, and addictions. So the negative statement is in vain. God is only good, and so the power of I am can only work in positive mind thoughts. To even state I am sick is dangerous. I am not the sickness. I may have an illness at the moment, but I am not the illness. I am well, I am healthy, I am filled with the energy of abundant life. Choose your words wisely when you say I am.

Allow yourself to breathe in truth. Watch what it will do; watch where it will go if you direct it. Give thanks to it. Embrace it with all your God Heart. Speak out and know I am. God is and I am and God is I Am.

Be still and know that I Am God. Be still and know. Truth will be revealed to you. The Spirit of Light is within us all. It is the spirit of the Father in the Spirit of the Self. Wisdom is waiting to be known to you.

Your true purpose is waiting to blossom and make manifest. You are the purpose of goodness, an expression of all life and you are love. Trust your divinity, allow your faith to commune with the Spirit of Light and emerge as a true Spirit of Life.

The universe is cosmically designed and mapped out for absolute goodness and well-being. If you are struggling, seek those who can help. Be open-minded and have the willingness to be receptive and to receive. The universe is calling, and if you listen it will begin to lead you to truth. Be open to it and ready to take off.

The innate wisdom of light fills our every fiber and vibrates every cell. All that we are exists from the seed of wisdom. A generating current of God Light that ignites the mind and flows through the nerves and cells as life vibrates and radiates from every direction simultaneously. We are nourished by the same light that fills the earth with the beauty, hues, and scents of a variation of plants; a common thread that weaves the transformation of loving food. From the slime of the sea and the dust of the earth, creative thought gave breath to the word in the imagination of being and wisdom brought forth in all its beauty and goodness God Mind in love, idea, and activity. In the allness of oneness creation merged the individualism of ideas: things that swam and things that crawled and slithered, things that flew and things that walked. In the I Am, all life of the uncreated creativity becomes form and purpose until it dissolves and absorbs back into the spirit of itself once again. We are Innate Intelligence and therefore innate mind and innate body.

Education is beautiful when it is in true relationship with the innate God Mind. When education stems from or ignites learning how to scam, trample over others, become coldhearted, dictate, and corrupt the ego with bad values, then education becomes ignorant.

Truth remains, as it has always been, untouched, unblemished, and unscathed. All that we conceive is but a discovery of what already is. We find it and uncover it. We are meant to tap into the infinite and eternal divine science of the Alpha and Omega through our own personal expression. We need to spend time with the internal self rather than just the external. We are to turn within and know the peace that the world cannot give us, a peace that is of the Spirit Mind, that flows in perfect harmony with our soul. To know joy and happiness in the moment eternal instead of grasping and consuming at the world is to live in the awareness of the inner knowledge of Divine Mind.

Is one better off living in a world of knowing the right mannerisms and how to dress for special occasions, how to act (think about the word act), and how to do and say the right things?

To be in harmony and at peace and full of grace is to be without any pretentious costumes or ritualistic rigidity, because whether they are blatant or subtle innuendos, they are meshed deeply into the subconscious. For most of us, there is a contiguous nature to all of the above. As my mentor had told me when I was in ministerial training, "We need to spend more time unlearning than learning." From great wisdom sprang the words, "There is a great sacrifice to be made and it will require the complete destruction of one's self-centeredness."

It is in the clearing of the way that we begin see and know that which was already there, that which we are made of. It is then we can begin to know illumination through God's deep inner knowledge, which we have begun to receive through unlearning the erroneous thoughts and undoing the lies.

We are meant to have purpose and a drive to succeed. One can succeed with faith and love. That is the true power. Though the negative may look impressive to bully or con one's way to the top. Looks are deceiving and illusions are manipulating. It allows one to function with a weak heart and mind and fall prey to the animalistic beast of the flesh.

The way of God is all power. God Power is our power. We are meant to be as one with it and move forth on a journey that is ours rather than a journey of being lost and trying to survive.

We have a choice. We have free will. Not a separate will, but a free one. We can take wisdom and filter it right into a state of abomination. We can duke it out and clobber one another like beasts trying to survive and call that power. If that is truly for you, then this book is not.

If you have even the slightest desire or an inclination of something calling deep within you, be it a disturbance that won't go away, or an insatiable appetite that is never satisfied, then give this a chance, or at least the benefit of the doubt.

I was once lost and lived like a dead man in the race mind of great limitations. Today I live, and at times I struggle; but I struggle because I live. I call it growing pains. Trust me, growing pains are much easier to deal with and learn from than rotting pain. Even in the hardest of times, once I have made the journey through them, I become aware of how they taught me and gave me strength. At the same time I realize, all too often, I struggled because of my ignorance and way too much of the suffering was self-induced. After all, I make the final decision about what to think and feel; I make the choice about how to react and respond to all situations in life. I and I alone am in charge of that. And that is a blessing when practiced in the way that is harmonious.

We are children of the Divine Light filling us with Divine Wisdom. It is ours to have, now, here on earth; here in this eternal moment. I Am that I Am. God Is and I am. We are one.

Exercise (Guidelines):

You may already be doing this. If so, take time to acknowledge how this is beneficial for you. If you haven't started this yet, please stop what you're doing and practice this method of meditation. Give it time. If you are struggling with this, or are having negative thoughts still coming forth during this, keep practicing. Often the negative thoughts coming up are you releasing the poison, getting rid of it.

- Slow down your breathing. Inhale while saying to yourself, I am. Pause for a few seconds and exhale while saying to yourself, spirit. You can choose another word, such as peace, love, well, etc.
- Listen to the silence and be receptive to it. It is the language of life eternal.

Part Two
Start a List of Positive I am Statements
Feel free to use this one, add to it, or borrow from it. The important thing is to get started acknowledging yourself in this truth. We are in the image of our Creator and our Creator is all good and so are you!

Say them all at first and then let your innate mind direct you. You may stop and meditate on one or several. Allow yourself to breath in the breath of life in all of its wisdom and grace.

Rejoice and Believe!

I AM
I am resourceful
I am intelligent
I am good
I am beautiful
I am love
I am loved
I am peace

I am wisdom
I am creative
I am open-minded
I am spiritual
I am clean and sober
I am hopeful
I am faithful
I am joyful
I am trustworthy
I am compassionate
I am positive
I am strong
I am grateful
I am happy
I am successful
I am understanding
I am giving
I am harmonious
I am enlightened
I am illuminated
I am empowered with my Higher Power
I am powerful
I am energy
I am light

eight

Altering My Gifts Before the Altar

Matthew 5:23-24
"Therefore if you bring thy gift to the altar, and there remem-
berest that thy brother has ought against thee; Leave there
thy gift before the altar, and go thy way; first be reconciled
to thy brother, and then come and offer thy gift."

Timothy 1:7
For God hath not given us the spirit of fear; but of
power, and of love, and of a sound mind.

John 21:25
And there are also many other things which Jesus did, the which,
if they should be written every one, I suppose that even the world
itself could not contain the books that should be written. Amen.

Humankind in the likeness of God creates in the image of His/Her imagination; in the likeness of all that is already in thought. Our church, synagogue, etc., is actually our body; the temple and the altar are our crown or super consciousness (Christ Mind).

These buildings represent the higher consciousness of our being. They are the places where we seek comfort in the divine. They represent where we go to remove ourselves from the hustle and bustle of daily living in the race mind and become restored in our true innate being.

Often many are left with disappointments, having expected the outer world to fulfill the needs of their wants and longings, and hoping problems would clear up or illnesses would be lifted.

The church is a great sanctuary to help one remove the outer world and commune with our Creator. It is a great place of fellowship and God Energy. But as long as we look for faith on the outside and make promises we really can't keep, insist that things be done a certain way or try to direct God with how we think things should go for ourselves and others, we risk the chance of not learning how to turn to God in silence. It really is about asking, "What do you want me to do?" not here's what I want from you or even what do you expect from me?

And when asking what do you want me to do, we ask not with confusion and resentment and anger, but with sincerity of wanting to be taught, trusting this path, knowing that faith is the activity of God already working in us. We cannot expect the universe to change just to fit our current needs. People talk about the chaos theory. Well, if the universe catered to everyone's confused and lack of understanding demands, then we would truly know chaos.

We who are spirit experiencing that which is of the flesh, revolve within the parameters of our human dimension. What we call a day is but twenty-four hours. What is a day for our solar system is well over a million years. What we call chaos is surmising that there is nothing more than what we see, rather than that what we see is a moment in creation that may take millions of years to evolve into what would then not be seen as chaos. God's plan is perfect. What we witness as beings on earth is but a minuscule of the Omniscient. It is in loving God that we then see only goodness and that we are very much part of the infinite design in the magnitude of Omnipresence. I rejoice in all that I do not know and in all that I do not even realize, for all is well!

It is in the learning through faith that we begin to awaken to the Christ Consciousness in us, to become aware of the Spirit of Light filling us with the inner knowledge of God's Wisdom, and to trust and expand on that. It is in the realization that there are principles of universal nature at work and that all living things are harmonious in this flow of design; a design that lives, in and of itself, a fulfilling life. If I want to eat I don't shove food into my ears, and if I want to walk I don't sit down. These basic principles come down to just being that of common sense. Common sense stems from the cosmic science of God Wisdom. If I want to become, then I must be. If I want life to make sense, then I must begin to know and practice God Wisdom. If you are doing it some other way and you find yourself saying, why doesn't this work, then I must ask you, why do you keep doing it that way?

We have options. We are not locked into "stinking thinking." Life is always in infinite and eternal constant change. A change that is all good. Change that seems to leave fear in so many is perhaps the most curious paradox of all. We fear change and yet, in plain reality, with each second we are changing. The most wonderful thing about life is that it is always in a constant motionless motion of change. Yes a motionless motion of change. This is not a typo. All that is, has always been. It is the Alpha and Omega infinite. We are witnesses to the Creator expressing that which is of His/Her Self: infinite, eternal, allness of perfect goodness. We are blessed that we are creative witnesses. We are of an understanding that begins before thought. Behold and know. Just know that the miracle is the blessing and the blessing is life in you, in this moment; this eternal moment of goodness.

That is law; therefore, it is a principle. Principles are tools of wisdom. We can apply them to our daily living and live in the harmonious flow of life itself.

We can easily fall prey to obsessing on the negative and ill-gotten solutions from a self-made foundation of negative illusions.

Since that, in and of itself, has no real power, its results, at best, are bitter sweet and rotten. It only leaves one bitter and full of resentment, anger, sorrow, and hopelessness. From that foundation one continues to build and develop an entire psychological and sociological acceptance of "here on earth." There is no "as it is in heaven" included in this structure of thinking. The most important part of the equation is left out. And then humankind goes forth and we influence one another with this abominated debauchery of life.

There are many recorded findings of primitive humans keeping the God of their understanding as a part of their psyche. They respected the earth and the sky and all living creatures. They gave thanks for their day and the nourishment that kept them going. Though fear played a major factor for their turning to a greater power, they knew and had faith; a faith that guided them.

Today, as humankind advances along in a great outer science, many have managed to educate themselves right out of their innate minds. The outer science of discovering that which already is, is neither good nor bad. In fact, it is amazing and brilliant. The unbalancing, however, is a disharmony. In the physical world, humankind has advanced rapidly since the twentieth century, but the inner world had been ignored.

Wars still continue in spite of the great advances in the science of weaponry. Hunger, famine, and poverty still run rampant in spite of all the science in medicine and education. And greed plays a big part in all of this. Great earthly profits are gained by the few, and many others do quite well for themselves while the true purpose grows smaller and smaller and the best of intentions dwindle more and more into a camouflage disguised as righteousness.

And why is this? One word kicks it off: fear. Fear brought on by the disharmony of living in denial of the innate self. Man has many false gods. Fear is the master of them all. It is the first things first of all that is cunning, baffling, and insidious.

The ways of the world and its problems still remain on a large scale. When has the human race ever come together as an entire global community and applied the science of wisdom? The answer is never. There have been some spots of global coming together. Even then, often there remained that missing equation. We did not create life. We express from it and take from it, and often with self-will at the helm. We discover and we create, and in doing so we are meant to give thanks with gratefulness and gratitude, knowing that we are in harmony as one in the supply of infinite abundance.

Too many religious leaders (but not all, by any means) for the most part are too busy hemming and hawing about who's got it right with God, accusing the others of being off track or flat-out evil. And they wonder why people are walking away from their faith; walking away from God. And that is the worst part of it all. The world is what it is, and though we may be in the earth, we are not of it. Our time here is the very small picture of a very big plan.

The church, synagogue, etc., is the temple of our outer world, but our bodies, our flesh are the temples given to each of us from our Creator. When we go to the altar of our bodies we are going to the crown. That is there we can commune with our Creator. We can just be still in the silence and learn.

Many ask, how does one do that? It is there before one's own altar that one must alter his gifts. If we have come there with unforgiveness, resentment, bitterness, vengeance, jealousy, and hatred, we need to take time to let go of these outer inherited responses. We need to contemplate and meditate on letting them go. We must start by discontinuing to feed them with our outer world justifications. These ideas of justifiable reasons to poison our hearts and souls will only lead us right back into an obsession with negative desires. It's like our own self-made feeding tube leading from the negativity right back into it. And when we have unforgiveness, resentment, bitterness, vengeance, jealousy, and hatred flowing through bodies, minds, and souls, in truth, we are, more than anything else, poisoning ourselves.

With that it becomes impossible to move on. In other words, we must let go of thinking in duality: good/bad and right/wrong. Instead, <u>discover your decisions</u>. Instead of sticking to them no matter what, let them be a pathway to a journey that's never ending. You may need to let go of a decision to see it as a path that brought you along in your journey and now it's time to let it go. Do not get caught up in the duality of it was wrong or why did I do that? The sooner we learn not to beat ourselves up, to forgive ourselves, to respect ourselves, we then begin to experience "on earth as it is in heaven." We become empowered by this truth and we begin to make manifest in this consciousness.

A woman I know had a very bad relationship with her father. When she was a child, his alcoholism caused much suffering in her homelife. They were estranged. Even though he had stopped drinking later on, he remained a very difficult man to deal with.

In his final years he had dementia, and his living habits were atrocious. He needed her to help him. At first she struggled with the idea of being a caretaker to him. However, she had altered her way of looking at him and began to see him more as a child; a child of God. Her motherly instincts (as she stated) kicked in, and she was able to help him lovingly. When he was finally too much to care for, she remained a watch tower for him, making sure he received the care he needed and was by his side right until his last days.

It's not about what we did or didn't do; it's not about comparing the levels of what we did or didn't do. Find that sacred place within, that true place of peace—a peace that the outer world will never be able to provide.

I'm remembering the example of the new crisp fifty dollar bill. The person holding it asked the surrounding folks if they wanted it. Naturally, most of the people replied with a yes. Then the person folded it and asked, "Do you still want it?" Again the audience replied with a yes. Folding it several times, the speaker asked the question again and received the same answer. At that point, the person crumpled up the bill, threw it to the floor, and stomped repeatedly on it. And when the question was asked again, still the audience replied, yes, they wanted that fifty dollar bill.

Why? Though the new crisp fifty dollar bill was now all crumpled up and worn and dirty, its value still remained the same. That cannot be changed by life's outer experiences. The innate self knows not of duality or man's laws. It only knows God's Goodness.

It is here that we turn to the Mother/Father with a desire to be in the image of our Creator. Our Creator is nonblaming and pure and perfect love, grace, peace, knowledge, wisdom, joy, and life.

God is all good, all knowing, and all power. What seems like a mountain of problems and an endless abyss of hopelessness is not even a speck of dust in God Consciousness. And we are of that consciousness. Listen to the guidance within speaking to you. It is the Spirit of Light and Life. Let go and forgive, allowing your mind and all your being to be cleansed of the erroneous thinking that only fills you with negative pain. Move beyond it, for you are so much more. You have an opportunity to truly awaken and never be guided by such lack and limitations ever again.

There was a time in my life when illness was starting to get the best of me simply because I allowed it to do so. Diabetes was wreaking havoc in me. My blood sugar was way up, and I was struggling with neuropathy and retinopathy.
I was going for eye surgery every couple of months. The possibility of losing my sight was a possible reality. Though I stayed in faith

that I was well and that I was already healed, nonetheless, it was getting worse. It was affecting my overall health, including my heart and kidneys. It was causing a lack of energy and creating depression due to the state of my physical body. I would struggle with all my faith to snap out of the depression and lack of energy, which would work, but that in and of itself was exhausting. I knew I couldn't keep it up, but my faith remained strong. I would not succumb to it. I prayed, asking for guidance: How am I lacking in prayer in my receptivity of God's universal goodness?

Then what came to me in several messages was that all God created was good. In other words, all that God made works to supply abundantly as one. I realized I was limiting myself in the idea of praying in the knowledge that all is well in me. It is all well in all that is. The universe is always supplying abundantly. I needed to become more aware of what was going on around me. It was in the infinite source that I needed to be conscious of the law of expression and the law of attraction. I needed to expand and move beyond my limited perception of these laws. If I couldn't just heal on my own in the oneship of God, then I could heal in the oneship of God's Universe.

My faith was beginning to dwindle. I was practicing walking around the house with my eyes closed, and the neuropathy in my legs and feet, at times, was really painful, even with the medication I was on that was meant to relieve me of the pain.

I regained my strength in faith and reached out to the universe. Then it happened. One day I was talking to a friend who also had type 2 diabetes. She was really having a tough go of it. As we were talking, a women came over, who I had just been introduced to earlier that evening. She handed us each a piece of paper with a name and phone number on it and said, "Call this person. He has a great reputation for reversing type 2 diabetes through supplements and a diet designed for your body's needs in good health." So I did call and sure enough, through the supplements and diet plan geared for my body's needs, the diabetes reversed itself. My eyes healed up quite nicely, the neuropathy cleared rather well, and my blood count dropped down to a healthy space. The inside of my body reversed itself, and to quote my medical doctor, the inside of my body restored itself to that of a healthy twenty-five-year-old male. I am sixty now.

The law of expression and the law of attraction are one. One cannot work without the other. Today I continue to exercise and I have taken up yoga and tai chi. My energy level is amazing. All of this has come into my life, and each plays an important part in good health and wellness.

I became receptive to a universe that is calling and I listened and I heard. I remain teachable. I became receptive and willing to receive God's gift through the wonderful talents of others. I accepted God's beautiful blessing of wellness by taking the action and doing the work.

Here at the altar we put down our gifts and alter ourselves in forgiveness and let Divine Love fill our hearts and souls and become witnesses to the true inner peace, strength, and courage that wait for us to make manifest. It is here that we can always return, no matter what we have done or did not do, and replenish ourselves. It is here that we return to forgiveness itself. For in this state, this plane, this truth, to come to it is to be receptive; to walk into it with our minds, hearts, souls, and strength to become in the likeness of our Mother/Father who art in heaven.

Do not wait for it to happen; that is another illusion. It takes place when you become the action. It awaits you with open arms accepting you as is. It is here that change takes place. Do not let guilt fool you into thinking you have to work on yourself first before coming before your inner altar. Guilt is a cunning disguise worn by fear. Contemplate and meditate and trust in faith. Try not to manipulate what is taking place. Sometimes if you come out of it feeling not so good, that's okay. That is only the poison leaving. Walk in the goodness and your step will be of goodness as you express and attract in this true self. This is the power. Know you are connected to the universal intelligence.

Feast yourself in truth and starve ignorance. Be enlightened and become illuminated in Infinite Love.

It is here before the inner altar we begin to understand the true meaning of surrender and it is there that we now can move into and beyond the altar in Christ Consciousness.

Lesson (Guidelines)

Give thought to a situation that still troubles you or an unfinished goal.
Take the time to contemplate and meditate on the following questions. Afterward, write down what comes to you as honestly as possible. If you find that you have already been applying these thoughts to your life, please remember we are of infinite mind, and we can always stretch more into the goodness.
Remember when thinking of people or situations to include yourself.

1. Have I forgiven or do I still blame?
2. How do I understand "giving and receiving" as one and not as separate from each other?
3. Am I approaching the situation or goal with love?
4. Am I approaching the situation or goal with resentment or anger or both?
5. How compassionate am I in this regard?
6. Am I filled with any level of jealousy?
7. Am I vengeful?
8. How much does fear still play a part, no matter how little?
9. Am I willing to let go and surrender it over to God?
10. Am I willing to be receptive to receive God's Wisdom and love?
11. Am I willing to do the work?
12. Am I willing to let patience and open-mindedness be my guiding strength?

When asking these questions, also ask yourself each time:

a. Am I truly working this or thinking I am, when in truth I'm allowing myself to be taken advantage of?
b. Am I truly working this or thinking I am, when in truth my motives are more on the self-indulgent side and selfish?
c. Am I truly working this and thinking I'm being humble when in truth fear is at the helm, and what I think is being humble is creating limitations in my life?

For every cause there is an effect. How do you feel about the effect derived from the cause in certain areas of your life?

God is the only true causation. When we awaken to our innate spirit self, we begin to see we are in co-creation with God. The substance of God is within us and we are in the midst of it. In this awareness we awaken to the Christ Consciousness, filling us with our inner most potential creating a purposeful life to be explored and enjoyed.

Become empowered with truth!

2 Timothy 1:7 For God hath not given us the spirit of fear; but of power, and of love, and of a sound mind.

John 21:25 And there are also many other things which Jesus did, the which, if they should be written every one, I suppose that even the world itself could not contain the books that should be written. Amen

Peace and Blessings

nine

Surrender to Win

Matthew 6:33
"Seek ye first the kingdom of God, and His righteousness; and all these things shall be added unto you."

Revelation 5:9
"And they sung a new song, saying, thou art worthy to take the book, and to open the seals..."

1 Corinthians 13:11
"When I was a child, I spake as a child, I understood as a child, I thought as a child: but when I became a man, I put away childish things."

Surrender to win is the essential beginning to getting one's self out of the way of one's self. Though we have looked at this in the four laws in chapter six and again in the previous chapter, I feel it is important enough to review again before concluding this book.

Once we surrender, then we have begun to clear away a path of wreckage, mayhem, and chaos of illusions and erroneous thoughts, and to become open to receptivity and the ability to receive and create from our true innate self a life of purposeful meaning rather than illusion.

We are here for a short while, and it is a great opportunity to sow one's soul into a beautiful masterpiece of cosmic wisdom from the essence of Divine Love, centimeter by centimeter, and drop by drop. It is our first things first. At this nucleus we can have clarity and the ability to live in truth, and we can see when we filter and or mingle truth with erroneous thought.

Though fairy tales are cute and poetic license is necessary, nonetheless, how the universe works must come first because there is an illusion of beauty in many a poem and many a song that keeps a man down in his muck and mire and soothes in a way that allows him to stay in it rather than grow out of it. Look at how the negative words in beautiful poems and music dominate. They far outweigh our attraction to the strength of truth. So where did it begin that the majority prefers to be inundated by sorrows, woeful indulgences, king and queen baby stand offs, and poor me looping?

Let's retrace, in reverse, the four laws. The law of attraction is a result of the law of expression. The law of expression can only be from that which stems from the law of mind. So know we are at the beginning—the law of surrender.

When going on only the design of self-will, we are functioning on the law of great limitations. Comforting only to soothe the savage beast falls into the rut of pleasuring ourselves, and that can turn easily into an insatiable appetite. It's a continuous circle that expands until it explodes. It feels like growth but is, in all actuality, a slow burial. More drugs (legal or illegal), more food, more television, more games, more lust disguised as love, more fairy tales, more religion, more weapons, more sad songs and sad poems, more education swaying from spiritual truth, etc., etc. It goes on and on.

Balance is the key. We are innate in nature. We are spiritual beings. Everything is spiritual: the visible and the invisible; the substance and matter. In and of that we are spiritual scientists. We desire to learn, to explore, to discover. We thrive on friendship and companionship. We absorb at an amazing rate and we put forth that which we realize and express with our own uniqueness. The outer world is but only our garment, designed from our thoughts and God's creative thought process.

So, I will not say this is right and that is wrong. That is where the problem begins. Because we base it all on right or wrong. I will ask, though, where is one's faith? We have a choice in laws of great limitations or in the Innate Intelligence of all that is. How does one wish to sow their soul from ignorance or from enlightenment? Again, there is neither good nor bad here for there is no duality. However, there is a choice. God's will be done or our will be done. Do you see where self-will really goes? It's never really your own. It must first have a purpose, a place to begin, ideas to pull from; a foundation from which to build from. So is it a lacking law or God's? One cannot dwell in two places at the same time. We can hop back and forth but not be in the two simultaneously. True balance in its purest form is to know that we are in the earth but not of it. For we are in the earth temporarily, but we are not of it eternally; we are of the divine infinite Spirit of Life itself.

It is also important to know that we can always start over anytime of the day, even several times a day, if need be. I cannot emphasize this enough. To start over is to surrender. In the realization that all is well in spirit, to surrender does not mean giving up in the sense to have lost in a sorrowful way, but instead it means to rejoice and return to your divine and innate self, to know your true self and expand in its goodness.

When you surrender, you begin the opportunity to open the Book of Life; your own Book of Life. You are the only one who can open that Book of Life, for it is in and of your entire being and belongs only to you, for it is you. It is then that life is revealed to you in all its perfect beauty. It is then that we begin to take it in and rejoice in it. It is there that we truly begin to learn and unlearn, to relearn and return; we return to truth, to life supreme, to infinite and eternal love guiding us with the wisdom of the Spirit of Light. It is then that we can see that we are one. There is no separation.

As we begin to understand this formula of becoming open to the receptivity of a universe that is calling and learn how to receive in this receptivity, we begin to see it all is one. We break it down into a division to help us understand and comprehend, but it is only one. One word, one thought, one idea, one creative expression, one motion, one vibration, one action, one love, one wisdom, and one life. All good, all power, all science.

It is in the giving and the receiving that we unfold into the realization of one motion. The infinity sign is a perfect visual expression of life at work. One breath is to inhale and exhale. To do only one is to not breathe. Daytime and nighttime is as one. The earth does not turn halfway around and then spring back. Giving and receiving are as one. To only give or to only receive brings disharmony. When someone appears to only be giving and asking nothing in return, that is only an outer illusion. They are receiving the love that comes from giving. That is why St. Francis stated that it is better to love than be loved. He was talking about the outer world. The invisible universe is love. To know it is to know love. God already loves you, for God is love.

Who are the Father, the Son, and the Holy Spirit? God is the Father, God is the Son, and God is the Holy Spirit. What is life? God is life. Who are you? You are God in expression as you. What is the number five? It is five ones. What is the number one trillion? It is one trillion ones. There is only one number. Zero is the beginning, the invisible ether, the space where heaven and earth are void. One is the visible, where infinite mathematical equations surmount to the eternal truth of perfect beauty. What is number one? God the visible, biblically known as Jehovah. What is zero? God the invisible, biblically known as Elohim.

One and zero are of the One, there is no separation. One cannot exist without the other. One is the expression in perfect creative design of the zero—Alpha and the Omega.

So when we surrender what do we surrender to? One truth. All knowing, all supplying, all wellness, all wise, all loving. All eternal of the Innate Intelligence, our Infinite Mother/Father who is always there for us and will never forsake us. For we are in the likeness in spiritual divinity of all life itself; it is the cosmic stuff we are made of and this is our soul food. It is our inheritance.

This is our first things first. In erroneous laws induced by self centered, self will limitation we starve and are malnourished, abandoning the wonderment of our soul self, and blindly expressing great limitations through it. So we demand more, more, more, and we are never fulfilled. In this paradox we are actually receiving less, less, less. Life is good and meant to be enjoyed. It is meant for us to enjoy life, to have fun in it, to play and work in it, to love in it.

The inner world and the outer world are our zero and one. This is our dimension. After all, we are at a point in time where we are meant to be in the two, inner and outer. We have pulled ourselves so far out of balance that we see two, but there is only one. All is spirit. Matter is spirit. The inner is the outer for the outer is the expression of the inner.

Is it enough to just follow and worship God? Just make someone like Jesus a God to worship. And what of the teachings? Are we meant to just cower before God? Is that faith?

You can do all these things I do, was the calling from the teacher. To do all things that I do: Did the teacher crawl and cower? Did the teacher harm and deceive? Did the teacher make people sick and beat them down into a slithering worm? Did the teacher teach us to war with our brothers and sisters? To consume in a state of fear and denial? Did the teacher abuse others for personal gain? If that is what Jesus did, then we are doing a wonderful job with these teachings and we have truly learned how to do all the things that he did.

Of course, I'm being extremely facetious. He came here to show us our true divine being. Who we really are and who we can become and why. Back then he was not received well when the masses learned what He really was here for, and to this day, the masses would rather make Jesus, or for that matter any great spiritual leader, a deity to worship and beg for forgiveness in a moment of self-honesty, and to bang over each other's head for not believing in the exact same way. It sounds like there is too much of not putting away such childish things and instead allowing the savage beast to be soothed (*1 Corinthians 13:11*).

Surrender to God's Wisdom. It is there that love will fill your soul and replenish your entire being. Go forth in this knowledge; a law of perfect love and harmony. Move out of the illusion and see the beauty. See the Eden Consciousness. Surrender to truth and awaken to the Alpha and Omega of the divine and perfect motion of God Mind and God Expression. Be fruitful and multiply in this consciousness rather than in limitation. Reap the benefits of the ever-expanding universe of infinite goodness.

A few years ago I leant a guitar to a friend, who was a fellow musician. His guitar was in the repair shop and he had a gig. He needed it only for that one job. A few days went by and I had not heard from him. I left several messages explaining that I would need the guitar that coming Sunday for a church service. He didn't return the calls. Sunday came and I used a different guitar, but I had not heard from him. To say the least, I was starting to become rather upset. I called a few more times, only getting a voice mail. In addition he had moved so I did not have a current address. At that point my mind was becoming sour. I began having vengeful thoughts. I felt betrayed and made a fool of. The vengeful thoughts were becoming more and more, and the vengeful thoughts increased. I also began to blame myself, calling myself a real sap and a full blown sucker. It was out of hand. The out of hand part being what was going on in my head. So I began to surrender and asked God, "How do I deal with this?" I was making myself sick obsessing over it. I wanted to let it go. Finally, a voice in my head very plainly and clearly said, "Give it to him as a present." As plain and as clear as it was, that was not the answer I wanted, so I asked again. And again I heard the same answer just as clearly as the first time. I pondered on the concept, and I began to sway in that direction. So I said, "God, how about you give it to him as a present, and I'll stand by your decision?" But again I heard, with great clarity and a little bit louder, "Give it to him as a present!" I began to see the wisdom in this. If I gave it to him as a present, then I would have no resentments; there would be no blaming, no vengeful thoughts, only peace. So first I forgave him and myself, and then I surrendered to God's Wisdom. I called my friend again and left a message saying that I wanted him to keep the guitar, that it was a gift from me to him. But I did put in a little added note that if he ever wanted to give the guitar to me as a gift, I would accept it. So I pulled it off, well, at least 99 percent pulled it off.

The really good news in giving my friend the guitar was that I was immediately restored to a deep sense of inner peace. I truly let it go and truly gave him the guitar as a gift. Occasionally I would start to get upset and begin acting up with a resentful attitude, but a higher consciousness in me would say, "Now hold up there, you gave him the guitar as a gift," and I would immediately let it all go and return to a consciousness of wellness. God's Wisdom prevailed and spared me from so much self-induced anguish.

A year later I received a phone call from my friend, apologizing for having held on to the guitar all that time. He claimed that as more time went on, it was harder for him to call and make amends to square things right. With that said, he very much wanted to return the guitar and promptly did so.

Practice

- Surrender to win and know your way, walk your path, see in the glory of your purposeful and fulfilling life.
- Be a witness to your cup that runneth over. Be open to the receptivity of God's Universe calling and receive it through the glory of your innate mind.
- Don't let doubts and fears stop you; when you fall prey to them, return to truth. Return as often as you need to.
- Surrender them over to the Divine Intelligence of God, where they belong.
- Fill your heart with forgiveness; forgive others as you forgive yourself.
- Love all of creation.
- Do not let the illusions sway you.
- Feed your soul with the science of Divine Wisdom.
- Remain open-minded and teachable.
- Surrender to win and never compete again for wellness and peace of mind.

ten

Life...Living in Fantastic Energy

Exodus 40:38
"For the cloud of the Lord was upon the tabernacle by day, and fire was on it by night, in the sight of all the house of Israel, throughout all their journeys."

Matthew 10:16
"Behold I send you forth as sheep among wolves: be ye therefore wise as serpents, and harmless as doves."

There is no separation. A brilliant inventor/engineer once told me the center point of the universe is wherever you place it. I agree simply because God is everywhere. It boils down to what one seeks right from their angle and dimension of need and understanding. But it also says in scripture, "Knock and I will answer" (Luke 11:9). The better we know what to ask, the clearer we will hear the answer.

One can see Jesus as a deity to grovel before and petition with prayer. Those prayers will be fulfilled at the level of one's clarity in their faith. Often the prayer is answered and the person has no idea what happened other than, "It's a miracle!"

So why not know the truth? That it is our faith which is the activity of God already at work in us. And that activity wants us only to soar in joy and goodness. Our suffering is our lack of faith. Suffering, however, allows us to learn and grow. Wherever we are, God is there. God was always there in the first place. For all of creation is God in motion. It is only ourselves that abandon ourselves.

Jesus came here to teach us, to show us, to be the guiding path of God Idea. If Jesus in the human body were meant to be here only to do miracles then he would still be here, not just for some point in time for a few short years. We were shown who we are and how we can become, to grow from the root to the crown, to have a relationship with the universe that is all good and providing. The Christ is within us all; it is the spirit eternal working in us and through us and as us. We are one in spirit in an ever-vast ocean of creative expression. We are the infinite idea, expanding in harmonious love. Jesus came to teach us this, to wake us up and teach us who we are and how to light the Christ within and begin our journey from the root back to the crown.

All of life is God and in the creative manifestation of God Idea (creative thought/concept) all is wisdom: the science of God's Wisdom. We can grovel before it and beg it for mercy and forgiveness and expect it to carry us, and in faith so it is, for God is merciful and loving. However, we can also discover within that Christ Mind is ours to express and vibrate from, and that God's playground is our playground too. We are all invited to play, that is why we exist: to play with God; to sing and laugh and rejoice; to love and stretch and soar beyond the self-claimed squatter's center point; and to vibrate in God's Name, God's Word. All good, all perfect, and all one.

Surrendering is to let go and let God, or, in other words, to let go of the self-will that so easily runs riot, runs amuck, runs away from truth, runs into self-made brick walls; runs everywhere but to our true innate self.

For myself, I find it important to remain in this consciousness as best as possible. It is easy to return to the race mind and let the intellectual self-will take over, often in a gradual and insidious manner. Sometimes the self-illusions create an appearance as if we drifted away because the good works are not helping, but the truth is that our shadows are quick to create confusion, rearranging and blurring truth.

It's not about forcing what we are seeking, but to have faith that the path we are on is a journey of spiritual growth, working in perfect motion, and it is awakening us in its peace, knowledge, grace, and joy. Life is infinite and we cannot force truth. We can go for the ride and learn through the reverence of our soul, being fueled by the actions of our decisions. Our actions will demonstrate, from the innate mind, our true selves, purposeful and meaningful, receiving the cosmic wisdom of our Father/Mother who art in heaven. Who's will (wisdom) is heavenly on earth as it is in heaven?

It's about taking the time to breathe in and exhale truth rather than trying to consume or manipulate it. To give it space and let the flow of life's divine energy become realized. It is then that we see the cosmic nature at work in its flowing order, unfolding the riches of the kingdom. It has always been there since the beginning of all eternity. We cannot exist without it, for it is as much a part of us as we are of it. It is here that we come to understand that we are perfect beings in search of perfection, radiant and beautiful, fulfilled and blessed, loving and graceful, knowledgeable and all wise. That is who we are and it is who we are becoming in the likeness of our Creator.

You can seize the moment and shape your destiny. It is yours to mold, to build lovingly, and to have as many center points as there are stars in the sky. Are they not center points, each and every one unto themselves? Allow yourself to expand and soar in the blessedness of life, knowing the face of life itself shines in your eyes and upon your lips as the Heavenly Parent lifts up His/Her countenance upon you with graciousness and divine order, flowing in the light of wisdom and joy and never forsaking you.

Behold the Innate Intelligence at work within your Christ Mind. Hear the life of the indwelling Mother/Father and see the great peace and know you are whole and free. Soar beyond goals imagined in pure love, expressing in the power of I Am, the Alpha and the Omega.

Know this truth and set yourself free from all limitations. Connect to the infinite; trust in your faith eternal. Do not live out your life tortured and suppressed. If you are even minutely aware that something is not right, that something is lacking, know you are blessed, for you are conscious of your innate self and have awakened to your mind's eye. For many it takes that "something," whether it is big or small, but something that makes us question the universe. If we are receptive, we will hear it calling us to life beyond, and we will find a reason and purpose to move beyond the veils and shadows.

That reason and purpose will unfold and unfold in a fantastic energy of self-realization expressing in a goodness of love and wisdom, enabling us to see dreams never imagined.

We need not give up everything and head to the mountains to live in a cave. I am only talking about within. Family and careers can remain intact. But from within is a new resilient and refreshed self. You can still remain at the head of all that is truly important to you.

At the same time, if you are seeking to make serious life changes, that too is yours to have. Fear creates the illusion of being in so deep that there is no way out. We can pull up and out of that, and be lifted into solutions, from career changes to freedom from addictions. Even a complete life change. The universe is calling and its message is, "It is all good." All that you need is already there; it just is. You are complete and always have been. Discover yourself and know you are one with life itself and all the goodness that is in and of it.

You are not alone and never have been. You are in God's Universe. You are love and grace. You are wisdom and knowledge. You are peace and joy. You are a beautiful being filled with light divine, purposeful and meaningful.

Begin the journey and become conscious of the fantastic energy within you, for life is fantastic energy and you are Living in Fantastic Energy. You are that energy whole and complete.

Discover this beautiful universe that is longing to express as you, waiting for you to soar wise as the serpent and gentle as the dove, and live in fantastic energy.

Peace

Bibliography

Holy Bible Study System, KVJ. Oxford: Oxford University Press, Inc., 2003.

Goldsmith, Joel S. *Beyond Words and Thoughts*. Acropolis Books, Inc., 1968.

Seale, Ervin. *Take Off From Within*. Camarillo: DeVorss Publications, 1971.

Corsiatto, JoAnn and Cecil Corsiatto. *The Science of Living, In Class with Emmet Fox*. Eustis: Book Production SPS Publications, 2005.

Johnson, Miriam C. *The Open Book of Revelation*. Lomir Publishing, 1997.

Butterworth, Eric. *The Creative Life. 7 keys To Your Inner Genius.* New York: Jeremy P. Tarcher / Putnam a member of Penguin Putnam Inc., 2001.

Brooks, Nona. *The Prayer That Never Fails*. Rutland: The Divine Science Federation International, 1973.

Made in the USA
Middletown, DE
30 January 2021